Wednesday's Children

A Study of Child Neglect and Abuse

Books by Leontine Young:

Wednesday's Children
Out of Wedlock

Wednesday's Children

A Study of Child Neglect and Abuse

by
LEONTINE YOUNG

McGraw-Hill Book Company

New York • St. Louis • San Francisco • Düsseldorf • Kuala Lumpur

Mexico • Montreal • Panama • Rio de Janeiro • Sydney • Toronto

Wednesday's Children

Library of Congress Catalog Card Number: 63-23464

First McGraw-Hill Paperback Edition, 1971
ISBN 07-072559-4

910 MUMU 7

"Wednesday's child is full of woe"
—ANON.

Contents

Acknowledgments

Many agencies and people contributed to this study. Without question or hesitation they made records available to me, spent time and energy in selecting the data I needed, and gave me every possible support and cooperation. Already pressured with their own work they took on this additional demand with such interest and willingness that they made me feel a part of the agency family. Their concern for learning more about the problems of these families and more effective ways of helping them is a tribute to a devotion that has outlived overwork, low salaries, endless pressures and little public recognition.

It is not possible here to list all the people who helped but among those who gave so generously are Miss Margaret M. Kirby, Miss Margaret Reis, Mrs. Helen Young, Miss Edith Parker, Mr. Wilson D. McKerrow, Miss Anne B. Regan, Mr. James Grant, Miss Jo Ellen Gibson, Miss Jane Cartwright, Miss Rowena G. Sprout, Mr. Allen T. Zoeller, Miss Helen Levy, Mr. G. Lewis Penner, Mr. Leonard Heglund, Mr. Maurice Anderson.

I am indebted to many others who made this study possible. Grants from Ohio State University and the National Institute of Mental Health made it financially possible. The special help and unfailing consideration of Mr. Everett Shimp, Director of the Ohio State School of Social Work, were a continued encouragement and support, and I am deeply grateful to him. I want to express my appreciation to Dr. Howard Pepinsky of Ohio State University for his generous assistance and to Mrs. Grace Reiss of the University of Washington for her encouragement, generosity and willing help.

To Miss Djindji Russo, my assistant on the study, I owe not only her unstinting efforts but her clarity of thought and excellence of judgment that were of such invaluable help. I am grateful to Miss Evelyn Stone who gave her the leave of absence that enabled her to take on this job.

1: The Twilight Families

At midafternoon five days a week, ten months a year the streets of our towns and cities throng with children. Just released from the discipline and restraint of school, they spark the air with their vitality and exuberance. For them the hours ahead promise welcome at home, play, and food on the table. Most people take this picture for granted. It is part of the heritage of childhood, that supposedly carefree period of life. Most people are unaware of the children whose heritage includes neither the security of welcome nor the satisfaction of food. They do not see the thousands of children who are neglected by parents too empty themselves to give to the life they have brought into the world. They cannot imagine children tormented by parents who see in helplessness a chance to hurt, not a need to protect.

Two young children quarrel fretfully in a filthy room and a baby lies in a sheetless crib staring listlessly at a stained wall. A little girl of ten comes in carrying a bag of potato chips and for a few moments there is the noise of children quarreling over food. They are dirty and hungry. Their mother will not be home for hours. When she does come, she is likely to be drunk. Their father is little more than a stranger to them. They live in a cold and lonely world where love is only an ache of emptiness and the dream of today is no more than tomorrow's defeat.

An eight year old boy slips like a shadow into the precise order of a house that has the cold correctness of a laboratory. He is met with a blow that knocks him against the wall. He makes no sound; experience has taught him better. He cannot control the trembling of his body and his legs feel like rubber. The cold-eyed woman who is his mother tells him he is ten minutes late from school. What was he doing, looking for something to steal, getting into trouble at school? For the boy there is no defense, only his desperate fantasy that he may suddenly have the power to make himself invisible, to escape to a land where there are no people, where only the blessing of silence surrounds him. This world has taught him pain and terror and helpless rage. Only in dreams is there safety.

These children are not fictional characters, the creations of a morbid imagination, ghosts of a dark past. It would be a better world if they were. Unfortunately, they are real. They live in our streets, go to our schools, grow up lonely and alien in a world and time dedicated to progress. Many of them are known to schools, to clinics and hospitals, to social agencies, to courts. Some of them will grow up to go to correctional institutions, some to mental hospitals, some to drifting and economic dependence, some to create families like those they knew as children. They are the children of neglect and abuse.

For most people the idea that parents could let their own children go hungry, could torture them, seems as unreal as a horror movie. Things like this might have happened once, but not in the twentieth century; or if so, only in the backward places of the earth. Yet the truth is that families like these do live in our cities and towns though they are as unknown to most people as if they were at the ends of the earth. If they are poor, they are lost in the jumble of city slums or buried in some convenient category of general worthlessness that assumes child neglect and poverty are synonymous. If they are not poor, they look and act to the superficial observer like anyone else; only the few people who know them well are likely to realize that anything is wrong.

While occasional reports of child murder or semistarvation appear in the newspapers, these seem isolated instances. They stir horror and compassion in decent people, but fail to suggest an imperative, pervasive problem. The very unpleasantness of the subject gives most people an impulse to turn away from it, makes it easy to assume that there is no need for critical inquiry.

There has been, until recently, little but the newspaper reports of the occasional case to alert anyone to the fact that such a problem exists in any great degree.

Not the least strange aspect of this problem is the relative silence which has until the last five or six years shrouded it. Social agencies knew about it, saw many of the families, but tended to treat each case as an individual tragedy apart from any overall problem of major proportions. When they did classify the problem at all, agencies referred to the families as protective cases—cases in which children required outside protection against their own parents. Protective work became a minor specialization within social work, but on the whole it was apart from the main stream of social work concerns. If one spoke of a protective case it was not unusual for even an experienced social worker to ask "What's that?"

Domestic relations courts knew about the plight of neglected and abused children. Judges often had to decide whether to leave the children with their parents or to remove them. The schools knew some of the problem. Hospital nurses and doctors saw children that were brought in suffering from severe malnutrition or from severe injuries of suspicious origin. Social workers, doctors, lawyers, judges, teachers all knew a segment of the problem, but they saw it in bits and pieces—the individual tragedy, the specific family. For them it was upsetting and frightening to conceive of such behavior as a problem of any proportion, as more than an individual, occasional aberration.

Then, too, most busy professional people rarely have time to study the records of experience over any span of time, to observe continuities and discontinuities. For the most part, families with neglected or abused children have been investigated only when some crisis precipitated official intervention, and official attention was necessarily riveted to immediate problems and action. That the observed behavior might be a continuing phenomenon was not denied, but only now and then would one person know a family long enough and well enough to confirm it. Social workers change, families move, cases come and go in hospitals and courts. Few professionals had time or opportunity to follow one family over a period of time, to know what parents did beyond the immediate crisis, and to determine what happened to the children. A hospital might suspect that a child's broken arm was not the result of an accident, as his parents said, but there would be no proof, no basis for action. The bone would heal, the child would leave, and if later he had a broken leg under the same odd circumstance, he would not often be returned to the same hospital. Too much pressure, too little continuity, and perhaps as a natural outgrowth an increasing resort to a "let's-mind-our-own-business" attitude left the helpless too often without help. Children were without protection because most people could not believe that they could need it against their own parents.

This book is an account of a detailed study of parents indifferent to their children, who permit them to go dirty and hungry, unloved and uncared for, of parents who beat and torture their children, sometimes murder them. The facts to be presented are not pretty, but they are true. Every case described actually happened, however improbable or impossible it may seem. Only names, places, and other identifying details have been altered.

The study was begun when almost by accident I discovered this nightmare world within a world. As part of a quite different project I had been asked to read a cross section of case records in the public child welfare department of a small Midwestern city. As I read, I began to have the very unpleasant feeling that I had by some magic stepped into a different world, cold, despairing, and sometimes malignant. These records described family after family where children had not even the most elemental necessities for anything that could be called living. As a social worker I had been familiar with families like these for a long time, but only with an individual family now and then. Like most people, I had assumed they were rare, tragic and dreadful like other calamities; not a usual part of life.

There were children who huddled in cold rooms alone at night, who never had enough to eat, who lived in terror of the unexpected blow, who even in their sleep never knew when the violence of a mother or father might hurl them from a dream into a living nightmare. Many of them had been removed from their homes by the court, and many of them had been returned because the parents had promised to be different. Most of the promises had not been kept. Many of the records covered a span of years, and many different persons had been involved in working with the families. That was clearly part of the trouble. No one person had looked at the whole picture, had tried to put all the pieces together, to trace over the years through many cases the patterns of behavior of these families. Even my first cursory reading suggested that there *were* patterns.

Out of that experience grew a study broken into two parts, both with the same basic purpose; to trace the profiles of behavior of families like these, to learn what they are like, how they live, how they can be recognized. Are parents who neglect their children different from parents who try to destroy them? Are there different degrees of child neglect and child abuse that can be outlined even in rough form? How do these parents behave toward each other and toward their relatives and neighbors? Most important of all I wanted to learn if there were any clues pointing to how families like these might be helped or, in time, how we might help their children grow into adults capable of fostering happier families. I did not expect to find an answer to that all-important question. Human problems of this severity are far too complex for simple solutions. I hoped to learn something, however small, that might contribute toward the search for solution.

In the first part I was looking for the broad outlines of family behavior, those parental actions that occurred repeatedly and especially actions that repeatedly occurred together. How did neglecting parents talk about their children? Did their remarks differ from the way abusing parents talked? How did husbands and wives treat each other? Did some share their problems while others did not? Did parents who shared their problems treat their children differently from those who did not? In other words, I assumed that no human action occurred in a vacuum, that it had living connections with other actions and that those connections were important.

In the second part of the study I used these observations to fill in more of the details of the outline. Those repeated actions were more specifically and exactly defined. For example, in what ways did parents share and what was their specific behavior toward each other and their children? The most frequent actions were listed separately in a schedule, which was then used with a new group of families to find out what kinds of behavior wove together into a pattern.

The families in the first study were selected from a large Eastern metropolitan area where there was a diversity of cultures and racial groups. They were picked from the active case files of two public child welfare agencies in counties suburban to the city and from one private agency in the city that handled only cases of child neglect and abuse. There were 40 families from each agency, 120 in all. In the second study, 180 families were selected from seven different localities, two rural areas in the Midwest, two medium-sized (that is between 150,000 and 500,000) cities and one large urban area (over 1 million) in the Midwest, one medium-sized city and one rural county on the Pacific coast. All of these families came from the active files of public child welfare departments except for one private agency in the large city that handled only cases of child neglect and abuse.

Information was taken entirely from case records. Some readers may wonder how accurate this information is since it is second-hand, recorded by many different people, limited by no specific outline. If it were concerned with precise quantities or identical objects, it would probably not be very reliable. But human behavior is neither a precise quantity nor an object. It is made up of actions and the absence of actions that are always interacting and reacting to all the pressures and circumstances from the outside that we call environment. Since environment does not stand still either, nothing about human behavior is static. Yet the amazing fact is that with all the ceaseless motion, patterns do emerge and remain relatively continuous. In other words, though every individual is unique, each conforms more or less to certain kinds of patterns.

When, as in this study, such patterns emerge from case records independently set down by several hundred case workers, their existence cannot be doubted. It is stretching the probable to the point of absurdity to assume that all these people would show the same distortions in observation, the same lapses of memory in recording them. The significant fact is that patterns of behavior did emerge.

The case records followed families over a period of from one year to as long as fifteen and twenty years. Under all kinds of situations, through all kinds of crises, the records traced their reactions. If the controls and precision of the laboratory were impossible, the spontaneity and diversity of life were present. This does not mean that there was no artificiality. The intervention of an agency or a social worker in a family's internal affairs is, for our society, out of the ordinary, a superimposing of outside pressure upon the family's customary way of behaving. This was particularly true of the families in question, who did not ask for any such intervention and, at the beginning at least, usually did not want it.

All of these families had become known to children's agencies because someone in the community had reported their behavior. Complaints about them came from schools, neighbors, relatives, courts, hospitals. Far from being malicious reports from people satisfying personal vendettas or trying to interfere in other people's business (which do occur sometimes but are easily exposed and dismissed), these were complaints, more often than not made reluctantly, by people who could no longer bear to see children hungry, left alone, beaten, and tormented. Over and over a neighbor or a relative pleaded on the telephone, "Please do something about this. It is awful. Only keep my name out of it. I don't want to get involved but I can't stand to see this go on either." These people who called the agencies seemed driven by their own consciences to do something that they feared could only cause them trouble, that might bring down upon their heads more censure than approbation.

It is a strange paradox of our society that one may complain about the mistreatment of animals with reasonable assurance of public approval, but that no such assurance accompanies a complaint of mistreatment of children at the hands of their parents. The parents blame the person making the complaint and the community seems all too often to wish that everyone had kept quiet. The sad result is that a lot of harm has already been done before most of these families are reported. No one knows how many are never reported.

The families studied here came to agencies through complaints. The parents neither asked nor in most cases welcomed outside intervention. If they wanted help, it would be for some immediate need such as financial assistance. They could rarely understand why the community reported their behavior, and they were often angry that someone had "gone to the authorities" about them. From their viewpoint the real problem was the community, not their behavior. They differed sharply from parents who asked for help because of concern about their children. The parents in this study more often worried about what the community might do to them than about what they did or what happened to their children. The fact that they could so behave toward their children that outsiders felt compelled to report them sets these families apart as a particular group from the beginning. While only 300 cases were read and studied, there is a valid assumption that if they are truly representative for the whole group of neglecting and abusing parents, the findings on these 300 families will in most cases hold true for all such families.

The cases were selected from reliable, authorized agencies where professionally trained supervisors judged them to be generally typical of all such complaint situations coming to their agencies. The final proof of whether these 300 are truly representative will require another study. There is no reason, however, to suspect that other families selected by the same means would differ materially; this is supported by the informal evidence of the caseworkers in these agencies who found the outlines of family behavior depressingly familiar.

While only a broad, thematic outline was used in collecting data in the first study, the schedule in the second was detailed and the items were phrased to be answered by true or false. This did not mean that the answers were arithmetically explicit. It referred simply to the predominant behavior that was true or false for that particular item. If the item was, for example, inadequate feeding of children, it was marked true when the evidence indicated that this was the consistent trend of parental behavior. This was a family where the children were customarily underfed. It was not a problem of an occasional missed meal.

The parental patterns of behavior were traced by what parents did and did not do. While parental statements were not ignored, they were never accepted out of the context of parental actions. The Biblical admonition, "By their fruits shall ye know them," was taken as a basic guide. Records of parental behavior were obtained by repeated observations by caseworkers, supplementary observations by schools and other persons knowing the family, the official doctor's reports, and reports of psychiatric and psychological examinations. While any single observation might be fallacious, the concensus of all those available was likely to give an accurate picture. Some parental actions were easier to observe than others, and some items were in effect useless because the information was not available. Some items required more judgment on the part of the casereader than others and rested therefore on a more tenuous basis. For the study the most important thing was the profile as a whole, the consistent actions and interactions, the connections and relationships.

The question of whether these families are all alike was an important one. It early became apparent that they were not. In order to trace the differences, 180 families were divided into four groups: severe and moderate neglect, and severe and moderate abuse. For *severe neglect* the criterion was inadequate feeding. To eat is the most necessary and elemental of all human needs. When parents failed to feed their children, often leaving them to snatch what food there was in the home, this seemed to denote an extent of neglect that might properly be labeled severe. This was not failure to feed the children because there was no food to eat but failure to secure the food or to make it edible. For *moderate neglect* the criteria were lack of cleanliness or lack of adequate clothing for the children or failure to provide medical care. If these conditions were true of a family, either singly or in combination, but the children were usually fed, the family was labeled moderately neglectful. While these are not desirable behaviors and while they can cause suffering for children, they are not as elementally destructive as failure to feed a child. A mother might have a dirty house and still care for her children. She cannot fail to feed them and still care for them.

When either or both of the parents beat the children violently and consistently, so that time after time the results of the beatings were visible, the classification was *severe abuse*. The rationale for this is self-evident. Beatings so brutal and so frequent, with boards and ropes and even iron pipe, constitute abuse. When parents beat their children only now and then, that is when they were drunk or under some stress, and the beatings tended to be less violent, the classification *moderate abuse* was used. When a family both neglected and abused their children, this was classified as abuse.

With the families separated into these four groups the question was, What kinds of behavior, if any, are clearly related to what group? Are there four distinct profiles, or two, or only one? Are these families basically all alike? We have casually tossed them together in our laws and our work with them. Is this a mistake?

The next chapters are devoted to what the study learned about families who neglect and abuse their children.

For details of how the data were analyzed, see Appendix.

II : The Hungry Ones

A baby lies on a filthy, sodden mattress. There are no sheets or blankets, though the room is chilly and the cold drafts seep along the floor. Sometimes the baby cries wearily, but more often lies in dull silence. The turmoil of children fighting and playing in the room brings no response from him. He seems deaf and blind to the life around him. He looks ageless, with his shrunken body and his distant stare. Actually he has lived in this less than perfect world for only one year.

He was the fifth child born to the Lake family. The seven Lakes live in a three-room apartment which had been dirty and deteriorating to begin with and has not improved with the occupancy of the Lakes. Once it was painted but now the walls are pockmarked and spotty, the plaster is cracking in a number of places, and here and there the bare bones of the frame are exposed. The floor is littered with dirty clothes, decaying garbage, broken bits of old toys, papers and boxes and rags. The children, nearly as dirty as the floor, squabble and scream over a bag of potato chips and a half-empty bottle of soda pop. They seem oblivious to the dirt, the smells, and the disorder.

The oldest of the five is Shirley, now seven. She has successfully appropriated the bag of potato chips and is doling them out one by one to the frantic smaller children, each time popping one into her own mouth. All of them ignore the baby, silent in his crib. They also ignore the inert woman, sitting in a chair from which broken springs and bits of wadding protrude. The woman yells at them now and then, but mostly she stares blankly at the stained wall.

Mrs. Lake is not mean to the children. If you ask her, she will tell you that of course she loves them. If you talk more, she will also tell you, "If only they wouldn't fight so much. Then I get sick of them. They never pay any attention to me. I have a headache, they yell just the same." There is an aggrieved note to Mrs. Lake's voice, as if she expects the children to respect her aching head, or better, to give her a little sympathetic attention. If you point out that all children are pretty indifferent to their mother's aching heads, particularly when they are young and filled with their own urgent demands, Mrs. Lake will give you a blank stare. It is not a subject that interests her.

If you remark that the children are thin and seem hungry and that they might quarrel less if they were fed and cleaned up, Mrs. Lake might stir to a petulant defense. "I do try to clean them up, but they get dirty right away. I tell them to stay off the floor but they're right back there soon as I look the other way." Again the note of complaint is strong in her voice. As for food, she puts some on the table. They can eat when they want. You look at the table with its crumbs of bread and cake, at the dregs of coffee in a battered cup, at the two year old girl who would have to climb to reach the table top, at the baby who cannot even climb.

Mrs. Lake sees your look and again she comes to her own defense. "I do the best I can. If my husband brought his money home the way he should, if he'd help me with all these kids. But he says that's a woman's job and he works all day and he shouldn't have to help at home. He says he earns the money and ought to be able to spend it the way he wants. He gives me twenty dollars and says that's for food. Then he goes and buys beer for himself. He gets out and does what he wants. I'm stuck here all day long with the kids yelling and nobody to help." Caught up in her grievances, Mrs. Lake forgets both you and the children. There is an expression almost of pleasure on her face already aged ten years beyond its actual twenty-six. The children pay no attention. They have heard it all many times. The baby continues to stare at nothing and now and then to give a small, despairing wail which no one hears.

Nothing changes when Mr. Lake walks in. The children continue with their own affairs and after one brief glance ignore their father. He does not speak to them. His whole attention is riveted upon his wife's recital of complaints. Angrily he interrupts. "If she'd clean up this place and take care of the kids, there wouldn't be any trouble. I give her money and what does she do? I'll tell you what she does. She goes next door and drinks beer all day. She goes down to the bar and talks to the bums that hang around there. I work all day, and I'm entitled to a little rest and some fun. She ought to stay home and cook a meal for me instead of my having to go out and find something to eat." Mr. Lake is thin and short. His body is tense and his movements jerky. Like his wife his face looks older than his twenty-seven years, and like her, his face has the crumpled look of a petulant child.

Mrs. Lake answers her husband's accusations eagerly, reiterating what he has done to her, what he continues to do to her. His retorts follow the same theme, what his wife does or fails to do for him. Neither of them talk to the children although each accuses the other of neglecting them, of indifference to their welfare. Two of the children are crying but neither parent notices. Deep in their quarrel now, their voices grow shrill, and they search the past for more evidence to support the theme of their ever-recurrent exploitation.

What neither parent observes is that even as they quarrel both neglect the children. They do not see that the accusations of both are true and that this is the real problem. Like children they are concerned to the exclusion of all other considerations with what has, is, and will be done to *them*, never with what they do to others. It is a startling fact that a severely neglecting parent rarely makes any statement about what *he* has done. To do that, as even the smallest child knows, is to place himself in the position of the actor, not the acted upon, to relinquish the image of himself as the helpless and often hopeless victim of another. The vindication of that victimization, the endlessly adduced proof of its continued reality, form an important bond between the parents though each must in the process play both parts, aggressor as well as victim.

Neither Mr. nor Mrs. Lake were aware of this, of course. Nor would they have believed anyone who pointed it out to them. For each the monotonous series of quarrels, accusations, recriminations, were no more than the inevitable consequence of the expected misbehavior of the other. Mr. Lake was quite sure his wife would continue to neglect the house and children and Mrs. Lake did not expect that her husband would bring more adequate support home to the family. The behavior of each inflicted real hardship upon the family but it also, in their own minds, justified their respective responses. Mrs. Lake could not carry out her responsibilities to her family because her husband did not carry out his. Mr. Lake could not alter his behavior because his wife did not alter hers. Each blamed the other for criticisms from the outside.

Since most criticism concerned neglect of the children, the children became both a major focus for parental accusations and a magnet for unwelcome community intervention. The fact that their neglect was known by outsiders had precipitated neither action nor change on the part of the parents. How much it had been of any concern or even awareness to them before agency intervention is impossible to say. Certainly afterward it became a favorite topic for mutual accusations. In effect each parent insisted that if the other had behaved properly, there would not now be a strange person called a social worker sitting in their house and questioning their mode of life.

Mrs. Lake went a step further. Angrily she told Shirley, "I told you if you didn't go to school like you ought, you'd bring the officers down on us." Earnestly she explained, "I told her to go to school every day but she won't listen. She's got to do what she wants." Mrs. Lake was upset not because Shirley had truanted frequently and would quickly fall behind her class in school but because her truancy had brought trouble to her mother. She implied that Shirley had sought to do just that. Shirley, her thin young-old face trained in a blankness she turned to strangers, officials, and parental anger, said nothing. With the astuteness of self-preservation she hid in the noncommittal refuge of silence. If you had told Mrs. Lake that she was in effect blaming the children for her neglect of them, she would have responded with self-defense, but it is doubtful that she would have understood what you meant.

Were these parents mentally retarded? In this particular case, they were not. Were they monsters, particular specimens of inhumanity? Or were they what has been popularly known as "worthless" people born to be "no good?" They behaved as a matter of fact not like monsters but precisely like small children. What was monstrous was the incongruity of their behavior with their age and their status as parents. Small children, when they fight, blame each other with a fine abandon. Small children when subjected to adult interrogation on unpleasant subjects blame the handiest person or even object around. They are not responsive to any logical exposition of their behavior. No sensible person would ask them to be responsible for the care of others. No one expects young children to behave in adult fashion, but nearly everyone expects parents to do so. The behavior of the Lakes denied the simplest expectations of adult society.

It is relevant to examine what kind of families Mr. and Mrs. Lake had themselves grown up with. Mrs. Lake was one of nine children. Her father traveled with carnivals, selling cheap souvenirs, and usually the family moved with him. Mrs. Lake went to a different school almost every year. Sometimes when business was worse than usual, the parents asked the local child welfare agency to place the children temporarily. Mrs. Lake was in four foster homes in a period of two years. One of the foster families became genuinely fond of her. She was in the eighth grade that year and for the first and only time she was on the school honor roll. Then her family moved again and she with them.

When she was sixteen, she eloped with Mr. Lake. As she explained to the caseworker, it was not exactly an elopement. Her sister went with her, and her mother knew about it. In fact, "My mother wanted it even before I did." Her mother felt there was no need to notify her father, who was then "away." Mrs. Lake added, "I didn't mind. My people never interfered with anything we wanted to do. My mother knew I'd do what I wanted anyway. She couldn't stop me." She and Mr. Lake were legally married, and her family moved on. After the babies began to come Mr. Lake drank more heavily.

Mr. Lake was the youngest child of five. His mother ran away when he was small, and his father drank heavily. Nevertheless his father worked with fair regularity, mostly doing farm jobs. Mr. Lake says he was his father's favorite and rather boastfully adds, "He always gave in to me. He let me do whatever I wanted." He explained with pride that his father came from a good family and finished high school. He never talked about his mother, not even to tell if she was still alive. Perhaps he did not know. He never talked about his brothers and sisters either. The record noted that an older sister had been arrested for prostitution and that her children had been removed by court action. No other information was recorded on the family. Mr. Lake's father occasionally came to visit the Lake family, but the visits were not happy ones. He was often drunk, and he fought bitterly with Mrs. Lake. When he heard that a social worker was coming into the home, he told his son, "You've got a right to do what you want with your own children. They're your property." Mr. Lake, Senior, was not aware that he was expressing a point of view that was old when the Romans held it.

Whatever had caused the behavior of Mr. and Mrs. Lake, it is almost a certainty that they had known little in their own childhood that differed from that which they now provided for their children. Both of these parents emphasized that they had done as they pleased as children, and unwittingly both had described a childhood marked by parental indifference. Doing what they pleased had been small consolation for the loneliness and anxiety of tracing an uncertain path between the indifference at home and the potentially dangerous and often unexpected retaliation of the alien world outside. They were still so wrapped in the cocoon of their past that they were blind to the nearly identical one they were spinning for their children. The tension of Shirley's thin body went unnoticed and the listless baby in the crib stirred no echoes of compassion.

This picture, then, is neglect. There is no visible parental attempt to hurt the children, very probably no active wish to

do so. There is rather an immersion in self-need so total that
everyone and everything outside it are only dimly perceived
like the blur of figures on shore to the swimmer under water.
The children with their own needs intrude upon that self-
immersion as irritants. They require physical care, guidance and
control, attention and affection, patience and forethought—all
the qualities that the parents are themselves futilely demanding
from each other or from a denying world. Most of all the
children require continuity. Their needs take no holidays, and
so they seem insatiable and endless. For the strongest parent
this is sometimes a terrifying weight. For parents like the Lakes
it is crushing or would be except for their insulation of indifference.

Continuity of effort, of responsibility, requires strength and
some degree of structure. Continuously carried responsibility
must fit the strength of a person, like an old coat so adapted to
the lines and curves of its owner that its weight is scarcely
noticed. It fits and it is warm and comfortable and familiar.
When responsibility remains like a coat too heavy, too stiff,
that hampers and binds, that pinches and tires, it is usually worn
only under compulsion. For neglecting parents continuing responsibility is a coat that imprisons far oftener than it protects.
They live out the fatal fallacy that to have a child, to assume
responsibility is to grow up and to solve marital problems.
Neglecting parents give all too vivid evidence of how disastrous
this can be.

Some of the parents in this study did from time to time
make an effort to lift the weight of their self-incurred responsibility. Sometimes this effort was precipitated by community
intervention—the threat of court action, or the encouragement of
a sympathetic social worker. Sometimes it was the result of a
rather desperate hope that acute unhappiness could be changed,
that a dream could come true.

Mr. White had such a dream. He had grown up in an institution and had never known his parents who had deserted him
when he was small. Out of his loneliness he had created dream
parents whose love never failed, whose only thoughts were of
him. When he was grown, the realities of life mocked his

dream. He found it hard to keep a job. Something always happened to hurt and upset him. His boss was harsh, a fellow worker ridiculed him or exploited his uncertainty. With increasing regularity he resorted to getting drunk to blot out reality. This frequently cost him his job, and the whole weary cycle began again.

He married a harsh woman who rapidly began to despise him. Three children were born and then Mrs. White left home. At that point Mr. White decided he would stay home, ask for public assistance and care for his children. Here was his chance to make the home he had never had—he was determined that his children should not grow up in an institution as he had. Mr. White tried very hard and for a time he managed quite well. What defeated him was the requirement of continuity. When the needs of the family became too much for him, he would go out and get drunk. Afterward he would promise himself that it was the last time it would happen. Instead, he drank more frequently, and his neglect of the children became more blatant. Finally they were removed from his custody and placed in foster homes. Mr. White could manage to carry responsibility for short periods of time, but it never became comfortable for him. When the coat pinched too much, he escaped into alcohol.

Carrying responsibility, fulfilling obligations, planning for the future, are actions. They require a goal, a direction, and the active effort to move in that direction. Without continuity of effort there can be no direction and without planned action there can be no progression. Inherent in neglect is a lack of continuity and therefore direction; without direction parental action is likely to be little more than blundering in the dark. The neglecting parents in this study did not plan and so their lives and the lives of their children showed no consistent direction except for the drift toward personal and family disintegration. What actions they did take were nearly always those impulsive responses to pressures and problems that seek escape not solution. For the rest the parents drifted passively, convinced of their helplessness and of the hostility of the outside world.

The outside world, it is true, has been and usually is hostile to them. Mr. West as one of eight children had to fight for what little he could get for himself in his own childhood. His mother drank heavily and his father was only periodically home. By the age of thirteen he had learned to acquire some of the things he wanted by stealing and as a result spent some time in a correctional school. Before he was out of his teens he married, and a few years later he deserted his wife and two children. Presently he married again, whether with the intervening formality of a divorce is not clear. With five children born to this marriage Mr. West continued his impulsive, erratic drifting which now involved his whole family.

His wife accused him bitterly of failure to support them, only to reverse herself when he found a new job which she was convinced would be the answer to all their problems. When this job was in turn lost, she reverted again to accusations, asking the child welfare agency for financial help since the family could not depend on Mr. West. As the years passed and the number of children grew, Mr. West's periods of employment shrank. He ran up bills he could never hope to pay, he gambled hoping to make enough money at once to solve his difficulties and instead adding further to them. He had frequent illnesses and accidents and was often in the hospital.

Mrs. West alternately berated and defended him. For her each new job was going to be different. In the meantime the family lived in miserable, overcrowded quarters and even from these were evicted for failure to pay the rent. Mrs. West talked about leaving her husband and taking the children with her. She pointed out with undeniable logic that both she and the children would have more security and less deprivation with an ADC [Aid to Dependent Children] grant. The plan never left the stage of words, and Mrs. West continued to quarrel with her husband and to make frantic requests for emergency financial assistance as the recurrent crises swept over the family like a series of giant waves.

Two of the small children went to the hospital with severe malnutrition, and the younger of the two came back a second time within six months with serious dehydration. For days the children would live on a diet of cake and coffee, and they cried from hunger. Mrs. West used this as a weapon in her long struggle with her husband and as a means of securing emergency financial help. Beyond this she seemed scarcely aware of the children's existence. Her husband was even more detached, and as he explained with admirable clarity, "I know I'm a mental case. The doctors have told me that. I know right from wrong but pressures make me forget." Neither he nor his wife ever mentioned the children except as proof of financial need.

Then Mr. West, more than usually hardpressed for money, forged a check. He went to prison, and Mrs. West turned on the gas in an attempt to kill herself and her children. She went briefly to the hospital, and the children were placed in foster homes by the child welfare agency. Three years later the family was together again and except that they were all three years older nothing much had changed.

It is a sordid story of lies and cheating and evasion and at the same time of confusion, hopelessness, and despair. Two delinquent children followed the impulse of the moment, married without regard for past or future, and brought five children into the world. But they had no idea what it meant to be a parent.

Along with their passivity, their confusion, and their impulsivity Mr. and Mrs. West lacked both inner and outside controls on much of their behavior. They were subject to the legal controls set by our society: when Mr. West forged a check, he went to jail; when they did not pay their rent, they were evicted; but when they starved their children, the children were treated in the hospital and returned to them. As an intelligent observer remarked, "A dog or a cat would get help right away. Only the kids seem to get no help." Legal controls in the sphere of family interaction and particularly between parents and children are not clear, definitive, or consistent. Neglecting parents think of them as illegitimate. Their attitude might be summed up by a father of another family, who, accused of permitting sexual relations between his sons and his daughters, remarked, "I don't see what business it is of outsiders. It's all in the family."

This assumption that behavior between members of the family is nobody else's business finds enough support from the society to blur legal controls and leave parents without the decisive structure that would set precise limits to their behavior. Since like children they tend to regard ambiguous or generalized limits as no limits at all, they often feel from their standpoint justifiably aggrieved when authoritative legal action intervenes. While no law condones the semi-starvation of children, in fact, the West children were so underfed as to require hospitalization and, in fact, were returned to their parents after treatment. While certainly Mr. and Mrs. West were aware that their behavior was regarded as reprehensible, in fact, nothing happened to them. This, to their way of thinking, confirmed their assumption that there were no external controls.

They knew also that no laws and no effective actions had appeared from outside the family to protect them as children. Both of them lived with the bitter resentments generated by their own neglected childhoods, and no one had interfered then. Some of the parents expressed this directly. They were in effect being persecuted for what had become, in their twisted pseudo-life, the normal way of behaving. They did not notice that they spoke with emotion and intensity about their own experiences as children, with the anger and grief still raw; and at the same time referred to their children, if they referred to them at all, with indifference and apathy.

Social controls were of course practically nonexistent: they belonged to a segment of society where such controls are not operationally effective. Parents in this group were already so socially ostracized that the threat of what other people would think could have little relevance for them—in that sense other people hardly existed for them. In any case most of the families they knew, whether relatives or neighbors, were apt to be much like themselves or already detached from them. Still, many of them knew that they were regarded as outcasts. But since they accepted this verdict with resigned passivity it could in no sense operate as a control upon their behavior. They might resent it but they could or would do nothing about it.

This left only one source of control, their own inner standards and behavior checks. Most of the parents were as deficient in inner strength as two year old children. Controls to be effective must be consistent and must conform to a standard that is itself an abstraction. Whether that standard is imposed from the outside or evolved out of internal character development, it must carry conviction to possess strength. To parents whose most consistent behavior was passivity, who had virtually no interest or understanding of any abstraction, who based their behavior upon the need or impulse of the moment rather than any impersonal standard, inner controls would appear to be a practical improbability—in fact the parents in this sample seldom showed evidence of any inner controls. Chaos was the result. Individual family members might frustrate each other in the scramble of each to get what he wanted, but out of this anarchy little but frustration and hostility could grow.

This is the bedrock of the confusion which characterizes these families. The dirt and disorder of the house reflects the disorder and confusion of their life experiences. A family uses the kitchen floor as a garbage dump, children wander the streets looking for a satisfaction they cannot find at home, a father sits in a local tavern and waits for his family to be evicted from their house, drunken parents forget about their baby and leave him in an unheated room in the winter cold so that he goes to the hospital with pneumonia, an alcoholic mother gives her baby to a stranger on the street and he cannot be located for days. The family rarely if ever sits down at the table to eat a meal together. Each member finds what he can to eat when he gets hungry, and the dirty dishes and remnants of food pile up on the table, in the sink, wherever they are dropped. Children go to bed when they wish on stained mattresses often without sheets.

This confusion pervades every area of life. The one consistent exception is the steady employment of some of the wage earners, the men who hold one job and in this respect are reliable and responsible. Strangely this does not carry over to other areas of life. The orderliness of their work life seems to belong to a totally separate compartment without connection to the chaos of their home and their family relationships. Accompanying the confusion in most cases is defective judgment. This is perhaps just another way of defining confusion, since judgment is in essence the capacity to act in accordance with an accurate perception of reality.

Because neglecting parents tend to wear the blinders imposed by their own unsatisfied needs, they can rarely appraise reality apart from themselves. Everything must be judged as it affects them personally, directly, and immediately. A case in point: the parents who bought a TV set on the installment plan and forgot they did not have money to have the electricity connected. The parents who are furious at a child because his truancy attracts official intervention to the family exemplify the same lack of judgment in another form. Even if they were not concerned with the child's education, judgment would have warned them that his continued truancy would precipitate official action. Yet the parents were unconcerned until the truant officer arrived and then they were angry at the child. This defect in judgment is a basic handicap that does much to shape the course of neglect.

One other quality is a consistent and perhaps necessary ingredient of this unhappy combination, and that is detachment from deep emotion. This may sound like a paradox in the light of the violent and frequent quarrels common with parents in this group, but strong emotion is characterized more by consistency, by endurance, than by violence. Shallow emotions may spatter like hot grease, but they are transient. They grow no roots. Even the quarrels between the parents tend to boil up and fizzle out leaving behind the dull resentments that may attach to anyone at hand. Even the hatred sometimes so vociferously expressed evaporates into the drab flatness that more than anything else characterizes the emotional life of these unfortunate people.

Toward their children the emotional detachment is predominant. They neglect not out of hatred but out of indifference. They do not embark on any campaign to hurt their children. They simply forget them. Sometimes they show a mild fondness for them, and sometimes they are irritated by them. In neither case is the feeling powerful or stable. Because the parents find responsibility so heavy they respond to dependence and the continuing needs of children as a burden that often they try to shrug off. They act as if the children were not there or, since they are, as if they should somehow meet the needs of the parents before they demand satisfaction for themselves. The woman who gave her baby away to a stranger was only shrugging her responsibility more directly and with even less control than the usual.

Detachment from feeling gives to these families the blurred quality of a picture out of focus. They lack identity as persons because they lack continuity of emotion. They must live in isolation because they cannot commit themselves to emotional attachment to another person. Perhaps this is one reason why they seem always to prefer to be with a number of people in a noisy confusion that can drown out the echo of emptiness. They know needs, impulses, desires transiently and recurrently, but the mature strength of emotion that makes parenthood more than an accident of biology is for them a room closed and locked. This is perhaps their basic tragedy, a tragedy that their children in turn inherit unless someone opens that door for them.

What are their children like? As individuals they are of course different, but as children of neglect they also conform to certain patterns. More than anything else they are searchers—searchers for strength, concern, consistency, searchers for affection, order, and security. In that search they may be appeasing or defiant, withdrawn or belligerent, sullen or flippant. Some of them, like their parents, detach themselves from feeling, from attachment to anyone, and seek in a futile indulgence of transient impulses a way out of their empty world. Others substitute dreams and live on fantasy.

With indifference and confusion at home, subject frequently to social isolation and ridicule from schoolmates, without access to that protected, prosperous world they see flicker across the movie screens, they have little reason to trust, little incentive to struggle for something better, little strength or structure to set a goal or direction. They tend to be followers, not initiators, easily discouraged, frequently hostile, often suggestible. The energy of youth is frittered away in all directions because they begin with defeat. Beneath the manifest behavior lies for most of them the deep layer of sadness that is so often present in those deprived of childhood.

A child expressed it in poetic words. She was eight and had already known desertion by her mother, rejection by her aunt, a weary succession of sterile boarding houses used by her mother or aunt as a convenient place to leave her. Removed from their care by the court, she was living in an institution. She was usually in trouble, fighting with other children, stealing their finery, defying authority. She was also very bright. One day her caseworker asked her what she wanted to be when she was grown. Her face shadowed and her answer was simple. "I don't want to be." When her caseworker questioned, she replied patiently, "You don't understand. I don't want to be. When I was very little I went once to a lake. I wondered what it would be like to fall in. I still think about it."

This then is the shape of child neglect in its more extreme form. The question that must arise is, then, are all neglecting families alike? Are there not degrees? What are their strengths? The statistical analysis sought an answer to the question and a filling in of the general outline with the specifics of behavior.

III : Profile of Neglect

The profile of the neglecting family was drawn by the items used in the statistical analysis, and each of these items described a specific kind of parental behavior. Thirty-seven of the items were truer of one group than another. Fourteen other items were important for all the families and were true of a high percentage of them regardless of whether they were neglecting or abusing families.

This does not mean that every neglecting family was exactly alike, or even that any two were. A profile describes the kind of behavior that was true for a high percentage of the families in this study and that might reasonably be expected to be true of other families selected by similar means and by the same criteria. Out of the 180 families so analyzed 34.15 percent belonged to the severe neglect group and 18.46 percent to moderate neglect.

All the parents who consistently underfed their children belonged by definition to the severe neglect group so long as they did not also abuse their children. From these families came the children with malnutrition, sometimes with severe dehydration, and with all the health problems growing out of poor nutrition. Their profile begins, therefore, with their behavior toward their children, what they did and did not do.

In the first place, when they failed to feed their children adequately, they also failed to keep them clean and to dress them with even minimum adequacy. The baby whose hands were so crusted with dirt that he could not move his fingers was a sad symbol of the extent parental neglect could reach. Children were sent home from school with an admonition to have their parents clean them up. Usually they cleaned themselves up if anything at all was done.

Their clothing was also dirty, and some of the parents let them wear the same clothes until they literally fell apart. Small children ran around nearly naked even in cold, drafty rooms. School children wore clothing that was torn and held together with safety pins. Sometimes little girls wore shoes or dresses that had belonged to an adult and that were ill-fitting and inappropriate. Other children ridiculed them. While most of these families were poor, they could have had more adequate clothing for their children. Agencies could and did help them. It made little difference to the children, because with this degree of neglect new clothes became old and tattered with discouraging rapidity. Ninety-five percent of the families failed to keep their children clean, and 98 percent dressed them inadequately.

These were also the parents who failed to get needed medical care for their children. If a child was ill, they were more likely to seek a remedy from the drug store than to take him to a hospital or clinic. It was from a family like this that a baby was carried to the hospital close to death from a combination of pneumonia and near starvation. The parents had still not asked for help or made any independent effort to secure it. The complaint of a neighbor saved the child's life. Colds, pains, poor eyesight, whatever the physical ills, were pretty much ignored or left to the initiative of others. This was true of 95 percent of these families.

Leaving children alone for any length of time is a dangerous business particularly when they are small. It can happen in any family when an unexpected crisis occurs, and it is rarely a matter of any importance when a mother is gone a few minutes. In these families, however, children could be left alone for hours and in some cases even days. When a mother habitually spent hours at a local tavern, when parents were gone at night until the early hours of the morning, the children were left to care for themselves as best they could. They were often lonely and frightened. Sometimes the oldest child was told to look after the others, and sometimes that child was only seven or eight years old. Sixty-five percent of the families frequently left the children alone for hours at a time and 29 percent had deserted them for days.

On the other hand, these parents did not beat or torture their children. Rarely did they refuse them permission to join in school and neighborhood activities. They were often excluded from such activities by other children because they were dirty and ill clothed, but the parents showed no wish that this should happen. They sometimes called the children ugly names when they were angry or impatient, swore at them, even expressed openly the wish to be rid of them. Occasionally a parent slapped a child, hit out impulsively in a burst of irritation, scolded and yelled. None of these actions are necessarily abusive, and they expressed the wish to be rid of the demands of the children far more than any desire to hurt them. Even so, less than half the parents behaved in this way, if scolding and abusive language are exempted, and they were true of only 54 percent.

The moderately neglecting parents were very similar in behavior but in a lesser degree. They more often kept their children cleaner and better dressed. They were somewhat more likely to provide medical care. While 44 percent of them left their children alone for hours upon occasion, few of them left their children for so long as a day. Like the parents of severe neglect they did not abuse their children or seek deliberately to hurt them. They might slap them, nag and scold them, but even this was consistently true of only a little over half of them. They were more likely to express positive than negative feelings, to give some praise, to indicate some concern.

Neglecting parents were not for the most part possessive of their children. They were willing to have them receive help from outsiders, make friends with an outside person like a teacher or caseworker. If someone showed special interest in their children, they were antagonistic only if that person was critical of them or asked too much of them. Like children these parents could react angrily if someone openly disapproved of them and get even by refusing to permit their children whatever opportunities were offered. Their legal right to do this was a means of revenge, some power to frustrate someone else. At no time were they very interested in continuing cooperation with outside help for their children when this meant effort and responsibility on their part. They were more likely to make such effort when the help was directly for them. This was less true of the parents of the moderate neglect group who showed more willingness and more ability to work with others in helping their children.

Unless help was offered by someone outside the immediate family, usually by a community person, and was maintained by outside responsibility, these parents tended to remain indifferent to the behavior and problems of their children. Forty percent of the children were at one time or another truants, and this was not just the happy escape to a day in the sun. It meant absence from school serious enough to elicit attention. Considering that in many of the families no information on this was recorded, the true ratio is probably higher.

The seriousness of this problem is self-evident. Children who are chronic truants are not likely to be good students or to continue their education. Over 40 percent were, in fact, failing in school, and again, information on this point was lacking in half of the families. Large numbers of the children dropped out of school with no preparation for earning a living. Particularly sad are those children whose psychological tests demonstrated that they had normal and superior ability. With opportunity and encouragement they might well have completed their education to become more productive members of the community than their parents. Granted that this would be unlikely to solve all the problems inherent in their childhood experiences, the structure and the incentive of success in one area of living could offer to many of them a confidence and an achievement that would make their families materially better than the ones in which they grew up.

With the changing requirements of our technological age, the old ability to absorb the ignorant and unskilled diminishes rapidly. They have become the tragic laggards in a hurtling society, the unwanted and unneeded. The children of these families become ready candidates for their ranks. The problem

of limited capacity would remain regardless of opportunity, but
there is no evidence that this is in fact true of most of them.
When, despite their home situations, they test psychologically
normal in intelligence, they may well have excellent capacity.
When an agency or a school or a teacher has offered them
special help and encouragement, many of them have responded
with eagerness. As one such youngster expressed it, "I'd like to
learn and to finish school. Only once you fail and fall behind,
you seem to go on failing until you don't care anymore."

Stealing and sexual misbehavior were frequently mentioned
in the records, but unfortunately the information given was too
limited and too haphazard to give any reliable account. The
impression left by the data would indicate that petty theft was
common and organized stealing rare. The children lacked standards of honesty, but they also tended to lack the energy and
purpose required of organized effort even in anti-social directions. Sexual violations occurred in the same casual manner and
illegitimate children were frequently a consequence as adolescence was reached.

Withdrawn behavior in children was more frequently observed and recorded than aggressive action. On only 23 percent
of the families was there no information. Whether the withdrawn behavior was more common or more commonly observed
by caseworkers is not clear. In any case, the apathy and depression of these children was abundantly clear. This was not
behavior that made trouble for the parents or for the community. It was the behavior of hopelessness, despair, and defeat.
These youngsters did not risk overtures that could bring rebuff
or initiatives that might end in defeat. They trusted no one,
and they expected little but rejection. In effect they withdrew
from life. Dreams must substitute for action, fantasy for reality.
At least in dreams hopes can always be fulfilled and defeat is
a fate reserved for the villain. But, dreams build no self-
confidence and fantasy teaches no pitfalls. These are the children who may in a few years join the growing numbers of
mentally ill.

For the parents the behavior of the children was perhaps
more or less expected. Many of them had quite probably shown

the same kind of childhood behavior for much the same reasons. The abnormality of the behavior would not seem so striking to those who had known little else and who had small basis for comparison. When they had been children, their behavior had been their own problem and now the same was true for their children. Certainly part of their indifference stemmed from this. Even misery and deprivation can seem normal if one has known little else.

If the behavior of neglecting parents toward their children could be summed up in one word, that word would be indifference. Children themselves, they reacted as children to the demands and obligations of parenthood and of adult life. They had little wish to hurt their children but most of them had small capacity to help them.

They treated each other in much the same way. Their roles as husband and wife, like their role as parents, were to a large extent abnegated. This was much truer of severe neglect parents than of those of moderate neglect. Only 19 percent of the former had defined their family responsibilities and carried them with any consistency while 68 percent of the moderate group had done so. When neither father nor mother have continuing family obligations, no one knows what to expect from anyone else. Whatever in the home needs doing may be done or not done by anyone around. If mother sweeps the floor today, that doesn't mean she will do it tomorrow or the next day. If father repairs the broken porch step, that doesn't mean he will fix the shattered window. The result is chaos. Family routine under these circumstances is pretty much a myth. To most people routine is something to be taken for granted—when something is around most of the time, there is no special reason to think about it. Yet dull, humdrum routine is one of the things that makes society possible. It is the traffic cop for the everyday activities, the time clock that obligates people to do certain things at certain times and makes it possible for other people to know what to expect. Only when something forcibly takes it away, do most of us realize how much of order and security is bound up in it. Young children know this very well and are as a result the world's arch-conservatives. They like to know what to expect, and being small and weak they don't take kindly to too many changes in the orderly progression of their days. There is a lot of comfort in the familiar, and the familiar is woven into routine.

Nothing symbolizes so well the confusion of neglecting homes as their lack of routine. What is familiar is disorder. Parents cannot know what to expect from each other unless it is disappointment. Children cannot know what to expect from parents unless it is indifference. In a sense their routine is a lack of routine. The familiar and expected has a lot to do with anyone's feeling of identity as a person, and these parents seem to have little sense of identity. Drowned in their own needs they are concerned with "I want" not with "I do."

Among the severely neglecting parents only 20 to 30 percent did any planning of their money, made any clear decisions and took responsibility for them, set any family controls. Even less did they share planning and decisions. Problems were individual not shared, and parents were more likely to quarrel about them than to seek ways of solving them. Few things about these families are sadder than their inability to share with each other. Husband and wife were worse than strangers. They did not work together, play together, talk together. Few of them knew how to play in any case. They sought escape rather than recreation.

The word recreation itself spells out its purpose. The healing of laughter, the sharing of fun, the sparkle of spontaneity belong to life lived with a purpose, with a freedom from insatiable need. Few of these families knew that freedom even as a brief respite. Even when they attempted escape through alcohol from the grim realities of their lives, they were more likely to drink alone than together.

One of the bright spots was an Indian family that had come to the attention of the authorities because the parents did not send their children to school. The children were certainly dirty and ill-clothed, but they were fed. The father had gotten into minor trouble with the law, and the sheriff came to arrest him. The mother promptly joined the fray and gave such sturdy help to her husband that the sheriff called for help and ended

by arresting both of them. There are certainly more constructive
ways of mutual help and one might take a dim view of sharing
a jail sentence as a constructive activity, but the great difference
was that they did want to protect each other and that they did
share their problems. They had some feeling for each other, not
just for themselves. When they were released from jail they
gathered up their children and left for more sympathetic
environs.

One of the hopeful signs for families of the moderate neglect
group was the greater number of parents who did take some
responsibility. In 68 percent of these families there was some
definition of responsibility. At least one parent made some decisions, imposed some family control, planned the use of money.
Disorder was present but limited. There was more routine, more
direction. Parents did not share very much, either problems or
activities, but one was willing to follow the other's lead. The
important distinction was that more often one parent was willing to lead.

Infidelity was not universal, as might have been expected. It
occurred in 69 percent of the severe neglect families and in 50
percent of the moderate neglect. Certainly the percentage is not
small, but considering how most of these husbands and wives
felt about each other it is scarcely surprising. These sexual
affairs were for the most part casual and devoid of emotional
meaning. Some parents were promiscuous, and there were indications in quite a few families that children were witnesses to
the sexual activities. A mother came home drunk and brought
with her a casual drinking partner. Privacy was not a common
characteristic in most of these homes.

While parents frequently quarreled about "other men" or
"other women," infidelity did not seem to be a major source of
dissension. The parents quarreled about many things, and there
was little to indicate that they felt more strongly about this
than about their other problems. Sexual fidelity seems not to
have been a virtue of great meaning to them. Perhaps their
very indifference to each other as persons made it less important
than it would normally be.

The loneliness of these parents is accentuated by their lack of friends and of relatives with whom they had any steady contact. Many of the parents never saw their own parents or other members of their own families, and sometimes did not even know where they were. In other cases, relatives appeared from time to time, often because either they or the parents wanted some favor or help from the other—help not frequently forthcoming. Usually after a short time the relatives either drifted off or left abruptly after a quarrel. They found neither security nor pleasure in each other's company, and each lost another source of roots in a drifting existence. The same thing was true of those who, under more normal circumstances, would have been their friends. They came and went with a monotonous transiency like people who collide in a fog. Mostly, of course, the contacts of the parents were with people much like themselves.

They did not seek out other people. They waited for people to come to them. They might accept or reject what the current swept their way, but they did not seek or decide or plan. The accidental drinking companion of an evening might be less than ideal company, but he was there without effort or planning on their part. Only in an emergency, usually financial, would the parents seek help, and in this they sought a resource more than a person.

There is a sterility in this passiveness that is in itself a human tragedy. The story of all their human relationships in the family and outside it is marked by what they do not do. The suffering, the deprivation, the destructiveness grow out of their sins of omission, not those of commission. Their emptiness mocks the variety and substance of life. They move and talk like shadows on a screen.

With such disorganization and confusion it is not surprising that there were few standards of behavior among them. A standard is by definition consistent, and it represents an accepted and acceptable goal. Most of these parents lacked acceptable standards of behavior for themselves or their children. They could not teach values that they did not understand nor give direction that they themselves lacked. Discipline of the children was absent in over 90 percent of the homes.

This does not mean that parents never told children what to do or not to do. The trouble was that they did not stick with any requirements. Their demands sprang more from the impulse or emotion of the moment than from any conviction or lasting intent. Without continuity and consistency there can be no discipline, and true discipline is education, a learning to comply with a standard. The children of these families rarely knew such instruction except outside the home, in school or community. Nothing was consistently expected of them unless it was not to bother their parents. The value and security of limits, the pull of a steady goal were a kind of security they had little chance to experience.

The lack of defined and consistent responsibilities for the children was part of this confused inertia. What the parents wanted done at any given moment and what they could successfully get the children to do constituted a pretty accurate picture of their concept of responsibility. A responsibility of one day was disregarded the next. This may have taught the children defensive tactics but it certainly did not teach them the meaning of responsibility. With their defective reality judgment the parents imposed tasks beyond the ability of their children when this was convenient. A girl of ten would be expected to prepare the family meals. Young children would be left to care for their own physical needs. Demands beyond the ability of a person can teach defeat but not responsibility.

Sometimes older children took on responsibilities for the care of household and younger brothers and sisters as if they found the vacuum left by the parents intolerable. This pleased the parents and they tended to exploit such willingness, taking it for granted with quick relief. It rarely continued to be a successful situation. The self-imposed responsibility was too burdensome and too wearing and the boys or girls, usually in early adolescence, found their own needs and interests too often in conflict with the never-ending demands of the family. Frequently they reacted with abrupt resentment and denial of all responsibility. The eager dependence of the parents must have quenched the most valiant effort. The meaning of responsibility, the pride and growth and achievement one feels as its by-product, were unknown to children of these families. The sharing that definite responsibility makes possible was closed to them.

This becomes a danger for the community as well as the children. Democratic society depends upon the voluntary and firm compliance of its citizens with certain standards of behavior. The confusion and weakness that result from a lack of self-discipline and a lack of self-respect can be quite as destructive as open defiance of social standards. The children grow up aimlessly; as adults they can be blown like weather vanes in every direction and following none.

When life demands action, they cannot act—they have learned little from their parents but modes of escape. The most typical responses to reality problems were to deny them, to run away from them and to submit passively to the consequences. There is in all this what amounts almost to an abnegation of living, an acceptance of defeat so complete that action becomes irrelevant. Defeatism is a spiritual poison that is passed on to the children, one that is too often encouraged by their experiences in the community. When they meet with defeat and indifference here, too, it is hard to see where incentive for change can come from.

Again the families of moderate neglect are less extreme in their behavior. They are not so likely to run away from difficult situations and while their passivity is a predominant characteristic, it is not necessarily so profound. With help they might be able to become more active themselves. The man who has trouble on his job and simply fails to return is less available to help than the man who stays even though he takes no other positive action to resolve the trouble.

Because neglecting families have so much inner disorganization, they have a particular and special need for strength from the outside. They need to belong somewhere and they need someone or something to set some of the limits they cannot impose for themselves. Church membership, for example, would provide some of the standards they lack. Unfortunately, in our highly organized society, membership in any group is not automatic. Our complex social structure has no means of easily absorbing families like these nor would most groups find them constructive participants. They do not seek out groups, and groups do not seek them. Thus 85 percent of them belonged to no organized group. This was as true for church membership as for secular groups. Even when families did belong to a church, the affiliation was usually more technical than actual. They did not participate in church activities and had little contact with its members.

Most of them lacked experience even with informal social groups such as get-togethers in a neighborhood. The parents seemed to lack the simple social skills that would enable them to join in such a group even on the most casual basis. In an experiment with a group of disorganized families the case-worker, after working with them individually, attempted to get them together for an informal party. One family had agreed to be host and details had been carefully planned with the social worker in advance. The evening of the party the hosts darkened their house and hid behind drawn blinds. The family had gone into a panic as the appointed time approached and had taken the most direct and primitive means of escape from the obligation.

A social group was ultimately organized but only after the social worker had not only planned with the families but had also attended the parties, supervising and sharing all responsibility. When these families had gained some confidence and some knowledge of social contacts in a group, they were finally able to organize their parties independently and to make contact with each other directly instead of through a mutually trusted intermediary. For the first time they began to enjoy a group.

There is no reason to suppose that the families in this study had any greater measure of social facility than any group of disorganized families would have. They had no way of differentiating between parties that derived their vitality from friendly human contacts and brawls that relied upon alcohol for stimulation and generated little but hostility. In effect they were as much alone in the latter as if they too had pulled the shades and locked themselves away. They fled from groups as they fled from all human relationships however diluted and diffused. In so doing they deprived themselves further of any steadying bonds, any contrasting pleasure in their nightmare existence.

While sociological studies have found that participation in formal groups tends to decrease with lower economic status and to be lowest in extent in the economic group predominant in this sample, this does not diminish the seriousness of such isolation for these families. They are in effect deprived of the one source of possible compensation for their inner weaknesses. However partial that compensation might be, it would at least offer a focus with some stability in the midst of general confusion.

Whatever the solution may be for these families, it will have to be initiated from the outside community. In the records studied there was little change in the parental behavior, particularly the parents in the severe neglect group. They continued to drift from crisis to crisis with little feeling even for themselves. Some of their children were placed out of the home, and on the whole the parents were relieved. In general their attitude toward placement of the children was one of willingness unless community criticism aroused their resentment to the point where they used the children as weapons to spite their critics.

While there was, of course, no way of assessing parental attitudes toward placement of their children unless the question was raised, it came up rather frequently with the severely neglectful parents. When the idea of removing the child was precipitated, it was usually on the initiative of an outside agency—the court or the child welfare department. Rarely did the parents themselves make any formal request for the children's placement. This may be one reason for the common assumption that despite their overt behavior they want to keep their children. Actually in those cases where the children were removed from the home, the parents tended to evade any plans for their return, and in action if not in words directed their efforts toward continuance of placement until the children were grown.

Their attitude seemed to be determined less by the loss of

the children than by how they were treated by the court and social agency. In one family three sisters were removed from the custody of parents who had dragged them from town to town, from slum to slum, from deprivation to deprivation all of their young lives. Unhappy, anxious, resentful children, they were already outcasts. They were lucky enough to be placed by the child welfare agency in a warm, solid foster home with parents who came to feel for them as their own. The natural parents were angry and relieved: angry at the public criticism and relieved to be free of the responsibility. They promised before they left for yet another town that they would have the children home again.

They did return girded for battle. The foster parents and the caseworker welcomed them without criticism, listened to their troubles and made no plans to return the children. Thereafter the parents visited whenever their peripatetic existence brought them near, and they enjoyed their visits. They liked to talk to the foster parents who listened to their problems and did not try to blame them for the problems of others, even when the others were their own children. The girls grew up there and they did well. Their own parents created no conflicting loyalties for them, and as grown young women they were able out of their own security and strength to understand their parents as perpetual children.

The hope for all these families lies in their children's escape from the endless cycle of confusion and defeat. The families constitute in effect a group outside of society, yet a growing burden upon society—a circumstance tragic for themselves as well as for the community. The families of moderate neglect show more strength, more cohesion, more capacity to respond to help from the outside than those of more severe neglect. With help they may well be able to develop the standards of responsibility, self-discipline, and self-respect that would enable their children to be more adequate parents, to initiate a new direction for the future.

The children of severely neglecting parents may require placement away from their parents or far more complete and active help than has yet been given them. Some people tend to think of them as hopeless. Yet the young still reach out for life and health. They are hopeless only when no one reaches out to them. To ask them to be concerned for the standards of the community, to strive for independence when the community is not concerned for their dependence probably is hopeless. The brightest spot in the bleak picture of neglect is the repeated indication that the children want something better, that they resign themselves to chaos only when the hope of order has been denied too long.

A thirteen year old girl named Ann showed what hope and a little human concern can do. She spent the first twelve years of her life with an alcoholic mother who was sexually promiscuous. Her father had left so long before she did not even remember him. Her life had been the weary coldness of loneliness and neglect. She began to haunt the city streets looking for company, something to do, someone to be with. More and more she truanted from school until she was absent more than she was there. She was failing in all her subjects. When the school principal talked to her she responded with sullen hostility and indifference.

The court removed her from her mother's custody and placed her with an aunt. The aunt was not by any means an ideal parent, but she did have more strength, more sense of responsibility, more concern than Ann's mother. A child welfare agency assumed the obligation of supervising the placement and trying to change Ann's way of life. Among other things they had a psychological test made of Ann's capacity to learn and found that she was of superior intelligence. A young teacher employed by the agency began to tutor her every week. For Ann, the teacher's eagerness for her to learn was more important than the tutoring.

The really important thing was that Ann could reach out and cooperate with those who were interested in her. A year later she was passing every subject, going to school every day, and finding that achievement gave her a sense of pride she had never felt before. She wrote an essay for her English class on a subject she chose herself. It is the best answer to the question, "Do these children want something different?"

STREET MANNERS

When in the street you must always remember all eyes are on you, your every move the way you walk, your appearance. Therefore when in the street when walking in two or three do not walk so the people coming in the opposite direction will have to come between or walk all the way to the other side of the street to get around. You are supposed to walk in a file line so that people will not have to walk further just to make way for you and your friends. Also, when in the street loud talking spoils the appearance of you and your companions. Profane language in the street makes people think that you have no home training. Bicycle riding on sidewalks makes it impossible for people there to walk without thinking they might get knocked down or hurt seriously, therefore we have special places for bicycle riding places. Fighting and other dangerous things makes it unsafe or dangerous for pedestrians. The street is not a place for dressing. Girls who comb their hair, apply makeup, pull up their slips or stockings makes people think you want to be noticed. There are other ways to be noticed in the street such as neat appearance, nice manners. High school children who have just come from a game should use caution, there is no further need for cheering, you have left the game and are on the street, there is no need now to disturb the peace. Running in the street is very dangerous, you don't have to run the world is not coming to an end, when you run you endanger others. When people are in back of you and want to get around move to the side if you are not in a hurry; maybe they are. Your elders are the ones you should respect. When there is an older person around and you have something to say to your friend that is not supposed to reach the ear of an elder, wait until they have passed. Boys and girls who kiss or boys who touch girls in the wrong places are not making a good impression. All of these things if you do them give people the wrong impression. If all these things were followed by all pedestrians the street would be a better place to walk.

IV : Parents Who Hate

A tall, well-dressed man sits in the office of a social agency talking to a caseworker. She has called him because a neighbor has reluctantly complained that he beats his children with excessive brutality. Mr. Nolan speaks with quiet emphasis. His language and diction indicate an educated man.

He is explaining that he loves his children. His wife indulges them too much, but this is really the only problem. Of course, the children have to obey his commands, and when they don't he punishes them. One evening recently he told his four year old son to go into the basement and stay there. The little boy went down the stairs and ran quickly back. It was very dark, and he was frightened. "I spanked him and told him to go back," explains the smiling father. "He went down the stairs and again ran back to the light, frightened, so I spanked him again and sent him back. He returned four times and each time I spanked him harder. The last time he stayed down."

"And what did the little boy do that you punished him so severely?" asked the caseworker.

A look of blank surprise comes over Mr. Nolan's face. He stares at the caseworker, and when he speaks his voice is for the first time uncertain. "I don't remember. I can't think what he did." A wariness appears in his eyes, and he remarks that his time is short and he must leave shortly.

Mr. Nolan was a successful man and well educated. He was able to afford a comfortable home for his family, and there was no financial strain. His wife was a college graduate. There were four children, one still an infant. Mrs. Nolan looked older than her husband, and her face had a vague, uncertain expression that was reminiscent of a sleepwalker.

When she talked to the caseworker, she was worried and confused. Sometimes, she explained, she hated her husband for what he did to the children, and then again she thought perhaps she was wrong, perhaps it was all right to punish children like this. Only he beat them so terribly for nothing. One of them accidentally stepped on the kitchen floor which was still wet from washing, and his father beat him until he was a sodden, quivering bundle of pain. Still, her husband told her that she indulged the children too much. It was true she was not so strict with them as he was. He accused her of favoring Donald, the oldest child, and perhaps she did.

Lines of anxiety tightened her face as she told the caseworker, "He wants to break Donald. I know it. Donald is like me. He doesn't need outside recognition. He gets his security from inside himself. He only needs to know I care about him." Donald was a bed wetter, and this worried her. He was getting to be a big boy. Her husband told her enuresis is normal, and she had been reading too many books. She thought the family needed help and sometimes she wished the court would take the children away and protect them. Only she wouldn't want her husband punished. She loved him, and she would never want anyone but him.

A wistful look momentarily softened her face. When she was young, she told the caseworker, she was gay and loved to go out, to dance and join in parties. For a few moments she reminisced, and the memory of pleasure, perhaps greater in retrospect, glimmered in her expression. Then it was gone. Her shoulders drooped again, and she said wearily that perhaps her husband was right. He told her she had never grown up, that she remained a child with little sense of her true responsibilities. The trouble was she would get so confused. She would think sometimes that he was right and that she was a fool. Then again she would get so angry, and not be sure he was right. Sometimes she hated him, and sometimes she felt ashamed for feeling this way about her own husband. He provided a comfortable living for his family. He didn't drink or run around

with other women. He was successful in his work and respected
by his employer.

Mr. Nolan saw no further need to talk with the caseworker.
There was no problem except for his wife's weakness and he
was used to this.

Not long after this interview Donald went to the hospital
with a broken leg, and his father explained he had accidentally
fallen downstairs. The neighbors said they had heard the father
beating him. Mrs. Nolan and the children said nothing. Donald
refused to answer questions. His face was white and strained
and his small body stiff with tension. At night he had frequent
nightmares and screamed in his sleep. He jumped at unexpected
noises; when someone approached him unexpectedly and without warning, he cried out and then was instantly silent.

A few months later Mrs. Nolan attempted to kill herself.
Her husband said it was because she was subject to spells of
depression. He had done all he could to give her strength and
he would continue to care for her. He would take over more of
the care of the children and relieve her of the strain and responsibility. He loved his children, he explained, although he
observed in an unwary moment that he hated Donald because
he was like his mother.

This is the outline of abuse. It is not the impetuous blow of
the harassed parent nor even the transient brutality of an
indifferent parent expressing with violence the immediate
frustrations of his life. It is not the too severe discipline nor
the physical roughness of ignorance. It is the perverse fascina-
tion with punishment as an entity in itself, divorced from
discipline and even from the fury of revenge. It is the cold
calculation of destruction which in itself requires neither prov-
ocation nor rationale. Mr. Nolan described in detail the agoniz-
ing pain and terror he inflicted upon his helpless son. He did
not remember anything the boy had done to precipitate this
punishment; in fact, it had not occurred to him that any precipitating act was necessary until the caseworker's pointed
question caught him awkwardly unprepared. This was not an
error Mr. Nolan repeated.

The one invariable trademark of the abusing parent regardless of economic or social status is this immersion in the action of punishing without regard for its cause or its purpose. One could reasonably ask what crime a four year old child could commit that would warrant beating him until he lay broken and sobbing on the cold floor of a dark cellar, but essentially the question would be irrevelant, as it was with Mr. Nolan. This was not punishment for something the child had done. It was punishment as an end in itself, without rational reason or purpose—not punishment to fit the crime but punishment without crime. Its violence created terror and panic for the child, but it did not teach him any rational means of avoiding that violence. Like an earthquake, it struck without warning, and this was part of its terror.

Discipline and punishment have all too often been confused with each other; frequently they have been twisted into synonymous realities. Discipline is instruction, a standard and a structure of behavior, consistent and authoritative. Its standard may be good or bad, mild or severe depending on a given point of view, a given society and culture. It may or may not make sense to another group with another viewpoint, but it exists unquestioned unless some measure of disintegration has set in. Punishment is, in rational terms, one way of teaching and enforcing discipline. Its nature is circumscribed by the requirements of discipline.

The automobile driver who hurtles down the road at eighty miles an hour and flashes through the red lights at intersections knows he is violating a law, which is a standard of behavior, and that if he is caught by the police he will be punished in ways specified by law. If the driver following the legal speed limits and stopping for the red lights were also arrested by the police and punished, the discipline of the traffic laws would degenerate into a mockery. Punishment divorced from discipline becomes a monstrosity. Yet it is precisely this separation that characterizes abusing parents.

Probably every parent has at times shouted at his children or slappped a child when he was irritable or worried or felt he would explode if Johnny slammed the screen door once more. Guiltily he was aware that he was punishing his children to relieve his own tensions, not to correct their actions. More than one child has astutely observed that parental guilt and collected rather handsomely for that outburst of irritation. Such outbursts are transient, impulsive, rarely inflict severe punishment, and often result in more distress to the parent than the child. They are human, comprehensible, and unless excessive, unlikely to do much damage to anyone. By no standard do they constitute abuse.

With abusing parents, punishment is neither a response to temporary parental stress nor a temporary aberration from the process of discipline. It is deliberate, not impulsive; calculated, not a rupture of self-control; consistent, not transient; tortuous in expression, not direct and instantaneous. The father who wrapped newspapers around his son's arm and set them afire, sending the boy to the hospital with third degree burns, was not motivated by impulsive anger. He could have hit his son in a burst of rage, but it is difficult to see how he could have contrived the torture that he inflicted without deliberation. The mother who rubbed red pepper into the genitals of her five year old daughter and then beat her when she screamed in agony was not expressing transient irritation.

This calculating, consistent cruelty without observable rational cause or purpose is the key which distinguishes abusing parents. Degrees in the extent of the cruelty do not alter this. The importance of differentiating between these parents and those who may at times be abusive toward children is self-evident. A psychology that can incorporate this blind, ruthless pursuit of destructiveness may have connecting links with other types, but it also has sharp differentiations. It is clearly different from that of the neglecting parents. Its implications for the family, the children, and the larger community are different.

Abusing parents can also neglect their children and, in fact, probably always do so in some area of life. That area is not, however, necessarily physical care. The mother who tortured her young daughter in so perverse a way kept an immaculately clean house and sent all the children to school with impeccable promptness and regularity. They were always clean and well dressed. They never came home to an empty house—their mother rarely left the home and almost never when they were there. They came to school exhausted, and while they were not seriously malnourished, they were always on the edge of hunger. They were exhausted because their mother wakened them at five or six in the morning and insisted that they scrub kitchen and bathroom, run futile errands, and finally gulp a meager breakfast as the school hour approached.

When they returned from school, the mother was waiting. They were not allowed outside to play, and in fact, these children did not play. The living room was a sterile, cold room lined with new and unused toys in neat and orderly ranks. The children might look at them, but they could not play with them. They neither laughed nor shouted, but moved or sat like frozen ghosts. Even the dog lay silent behind the fragile barrier of a chair. Treatment of this sort is also neglect, a neglect of the soul, of life itself. It is neglect with menace.

In some families abuse was accompanied by the confusion, disorganization, and physical neglect to be found in the families of the neglecting group. There were six children in the Smith family, and they lived with their parents in four dirty, miserably furnished rooms. They were all malnourished, poorly clothed, and physically dirty. Mr. Smith worked sporadically, drank heavily, and relied upon public assistance during the intervals of his unemployment. Mrs. Smith and the children were afraid of him. Apathetic and terrorized, Mrs. Smith made little effort to care for the home, and family routine was virtually nonexistent. The older children were given whiskey to drink, and one girl of eight told the caseworker she smoked "reefers," or marihuana.

The hospital record on this family tells a terrible and almost incredible story. Two boys were hospitalized for broken bones, supposedly the result of accidents, a girl for a knife wound in the arm, a baby for malnutrition and three bite wounds—human bites— another baby for drinking kerosene. Two small children were dead on arrival at the hospital, both of them killed by what were vaguely described as accidents. All of the children had bruises, scars, and bite marks on their bodies. All of this happened in the span of three years covered by the record.

From birth these youngsters could have known nothing but confusion and abuse. These children were removed from the home by the court, and Mrs. Smith defended her husband. She said she "loved" him, adding that he was the only one who could control the children. Later she had still another baby, and this child died also under mysterious circumstances.

Mrs. Smith's defense of her husband was not unusual for the parents in this group. Most of them played out a strange drama of aggressor and victim in relation to each other as well as in their behavior toward the children. The aggressor might be mother or father; there was no indication that either sex had a monoply on that role. Whether the aggressive parent selected as his primary victim the other parent, one child or all the children, the passive parent tended to defend him, to deny the realities of the family situation, and to cling to the family situation and to the abusing partner. Someone like Mrs. Nolan might finally seek escape in attempted suicide, but the more rational act of separating from her husband was seemingly beyond her strength. She acted, in fact, as if she were a prisoner for whom no escape but death was possible.

One woman passively watched when her husband burned their child with a lighted cigarette. Later she told the social worker intervening in the family situation that her "husband was so good with the children." Not until the father was in jail for desertion and vagrancy did she reveal to the caseworker that he had sexually attacked his five year old daughter, had prostituted his wife when he needed money, and had sometimes locked her out of the house overnight. She ended her account of the family situation with the hope that now he had been in jail, he would change and they could re-establish their home. When the social worker questioned the hope, this mother explained that she still "loved" her husband.

A father passively permitted his wife who was a diagnosed schizophrenic to beat and choke their son. She had been hospitalized at one point, and he had, against the hospital's wish, taken her home. He told the caseworker frankly that he knew she had seduced the boy sexually, that she threatened to kill him, that the boy lived in terror of her. Yet to place the boy and hospitalize the mother would be, he said, "like giving up life." The tenacity of this victimization that could sacrifice the lives of all three and yet prefer this as "life" is so perverse as to defy comprehension. Yet it happened in a large modern city with scarcely a ripple of notice.

Only in a minority of cases did the passive marital partner leave the home or, more accurately, run away. In none of these cases did the parent take the children or attempt to provide protection for them. One father who had a good education and an adequate income left his family and his job and moved to another state. His wife both neglected and abused the children, showing particular violence toward the oldest daughter who was the father's favorite. She insisted that her daughter, a girl in her early teens, take responsibility for most of the housework and day-by-day care of the younger children. The girl was severely beaten by her mother.

While the father was aware of this situation and openly expressed his preference for this daughter, he made no attempt to protect her or to work out any other living arrangement for her. After the child welfare agency intervened in the situation, he returned once for a brief visit. He told the caseworker that he had a good job in his new residence and would be glad to take his oldest daughter to live with him provided the agency would make the placement. The mother had refused to allow the daughter to leave. The father added resignedly that he wished the agency would remove all the children because the home situation was extremely bad. "Someone should do something about it," he remarked. When the caseworker pointed out that he was the one most able to secure custody of the children and that he had ample legal grounds to do so, the father left hastily. He returned to his job the next day without again seeing his children.

All the passive parents in this study showed one thing in common: they behaved as if they were prisoners of the other marriage partner, hopelessly condemned to a life sentence. When they left the family, it was in the spirit of escaping. They left the children behind as hostages and acted as if they had neither right nor power to intercede. Not a single escaping parent even attempted to defy the aggressive parent or to take any overt action to protect the children. They did not deny that the children were being abused, and they commonly expressed the hope that "someone" would take action—it was clear that they could not do so. Although some of them assumed responsibilty in other areas, such as in their work, they could not do so within the family group; their role appeared more as another and more competent child in the family than as a parent.

Most of the passive parents did not leave, and no matter how miserable the home situation, they clung to the aggressive partner. These were the parents who denied there was anything wrong, and when they admitted doubts, they usually retracted them in confusion and self-blame. They opposed placement of the children actively or they tried to evade the whole question and detach themselves from any possible action. In many of these cases the passive partners opposed removal of the children with more energy than they displayed in any other recorded area of their activities. One father, locked out of his house for three days by a psychotic wife who was known to be abusive to her family and who was clearly in a breakdown, kept insisting to neighbors and officials that there was no need for any outside intervention. His small son was locked inside with the mother who was convinced people were trying to poison her and the child. This father's explanation was that his wife had these "spells" occasionally and would get over it presently. He ignored the danger to his son.

The question of why the victimized partner clings to his prison so tenaciously is not an easy one to answer. It can scarcely be love, since he shows no active concern for the welfare of his children and he behaves toward the aggressive partner more as a prisoner than a spouse. It is possible that the children serve as a protective shield for this parent against the destructive behavior of the other. The more the children are the objects of parental abuse, the less that punitiveness may be turned against the passive parent. This would go far to explain their persistent and active opposition to the removal of the children. In effect, the children serve as scapegoats.

In many of the families one child was the chief target of parental aggression. Sometimes the other children in the family were abused in considerably modified degree, and sometimes they were more or less ignored, neglected rather than abused. Upon this one child was heaped all the hatred of the family. The abusing parent concentrated on this child, and the other children were encouraged to be cruel to him. The passive parent did not defend him.

In one family one boy was selected. The other four children were certainly neglected, but there was no indication that they were abused. This boy was systematically starved; the other children were permitted to take food from him. He was burned with lighted cigarettes, beaten with a steel wire, refused all treats and recreations. Finally, the mother attempted to hang him, and he was brought to the hospital more dead than alive. When his wounds were treated, the child made no sound—he seemed to be anesthetized to pain. When the parents were asked why they had practiced such cruelty upon this little boy, they could say only that he was "different." The mother explained that he did not seem to "belong" to them. The parents agreed without objection to the boy's permanent removal from the home. Whether they then chose another child as scapegoat or became more abusive to all the other children was unfortunately not ascertainable since the case was closed.

There was no clear pattern to explain why a particular child was selected for this role of scapegoat. Chronological place in the family seemed to make little difference. Occasionally a parent would remark that the child was like a hated parent of his own or that the child was the other parent's favorite. Thus Mr. Nolan was especially abusive to Donald because the boy was "like his mother." A number of parents insisted that the scapegoat child was "different," implying that he did not actually belong to them. They did not question that the child was born to them, but they thought of him as a changeling imposed upon them by some wicked witch out of a fairy tale. Some of them even used the words "evil," "born wicked," a "monster" "unlike other children," "like an animal," to describe their feelings about the child.

Human history has woven through it like a scarlet thread the need and importance of a scapegoat, someone to blame, someone to carry the responsibility for the unpreventable and unprevented misfortunes of life, someone to sacrifice, to appease those dark forces which disturb human security, someone who can be hated and destroyed with justification as intrinsically evil. Whether that someone be a harmless woman hanged as a witch in Salem, a Jew in Nazi Germany or a child in an abusing family, he is himself crushed under the weight of human madness. One wonders what the world must look like to that little boy who came to the hospital so immured to pain, so detached from feeling that like an image he lay silent and unseeing in the plain white bed. One wonders if he, too, believes that he was born evil.

In a few of these families the fantasy of the scapegoat was acted out with even greater completeness. Two children were chosen to represent totally opposite qualities and were treated in opposite ways. One child was starved, beaten, and deprived while the other child was indulged, not overtly punished, and given materially the best of everything. In one case the mother explained that the "bad" child was like her stepmother who had hated and abused her. She had given this child the stepmother's name. The other little girl, the "good" one, carried her mother's name, and the mother explained that this child was like herself. The hated child was four years old when the child welfare agency found her and took her from the home. She was the size of a two year old from long malnutrition and was too weak to walk when the caseworker took her away. The mother was intentionally out of the house when this little girl was removed, but she left the older, favored daughter to witness the action.

In every one of these cases where agency contact continued long enough for the recorded observations to be available, the favored and indulged child seemed to be more completely and disastrously damaged in personality than the openly hated one. When both children were removed from the home, it was the overtly deprived child who was freer to turn to foster parents, to make healthy emotional ties when given the opportunity. In one family with two daughters, the mother was abusive toward the older daughter and indulgent toward the younger. She had forbidden both girls any contact with their father who had fled. The older had the strength and resourcefulness to enlist the help of sympathetic neighbors in reaching her father, made her plans carefully, and ran away to live with him. The father initiated none of this but responded to his daughter's initiative. The sister, two years younger, feared to let her mother out of her sight, was a withdrawn, frail, anxious child who seemed, in the words of her school report, "dying on her feet."

Interestingly, in all these cases but one, both children were of the same sex. In the one exception, the older child, a girl, was openly hated by her psychotic mother while her younger brother was petted and indulged. This mother, however, insisted that her son was actually a girl, gave him a girl's name, and until she was hospitalized, attempted to dress him as a girl. When these children were placed in foster homes, the girl made an excellent adjustment, accepted the foster parents as her own and made it clear that she never wanted to return to her own mother. The boy was never able to trust any adult, fought the foster parents, maintained his ties with his mother, and told the caseworker that his mother had forbidden him to love anyone but her. Not surprisingly he was reported to be effeminate and confused.

In all the abusing families studied, the motif of aggressor and victim is present. Whether the abusing parent was the father or the mother or, as in the case of a few severely disorganized families, both parents, the concentration of emotion and energy was upon destruction. No matter who was the primary object of this destructiveness—whether one child, all the children, or one parent and the children—the theme of punishment as an end in itself remained constant. It was as if for these people only one aspect of life existed, and into this they poured all their emotional resources to the exclusion of laughter, gentleness, love, and loyalty.

This may explain the curious defect in judgment which so

often blinded even the most intelligent of them to other people's shock and horror at their behavior. With what seemed incredible naiveté they could describe the punishments they inflicted. Many parents said openly they hated their children. They seemed unaware that there was anything wrong with their behavior or that others might find it reprehensible; to them this behavior was normal. The more intelligent parents and those to whom the opinion of outside people was important learned this difference in attitude held by others and rapidly became more cautious in their statements. Thereafter they made an effort to conceal their behavior, but there was no evidence that they altered it. Even then, some of them could make such statements as the father who explained that he never left marks of beatings on his children's bodies where they showed.

The more disorganized parents who had little incentive to live up to the standards of any outside group even in appearances made relatively little attempt to conceal their behavior. Occasionally when their children had been forcibly removed by the court, they insisted to social workers and judges, in an attempt to regain their custody of the children, that they had changed in attitude and behavior and that they did love their children. When the children were returned, the behavior of the parents rarely substantiated these assertions. In one case a small child was returned to his mother by the court when she insisted she had "learned her lesson" and wanted her son. A few months later he was in the hospital with a broken leg. Among other things his mother had thrown him across the room against the wall. Greater discretion on the part of these parents often meant greater danger for the children—since most people are reluctant to believe that parents can behave in such a way.

The extent of the pathology in these families is more striking than that of the neglecting group and probably for most people less comprehensible. It is easier to recognize the reality of neglect than of abuse. The deliberate attempt to hurt and destroy one's own children violates a basic human premise. It is very probable that for most of these parents their children do not exist as people, as part of a family in the normal meaning of the word. The children symbolize two qualities important to the destructive psychology, weakness and possession. They are to a shocking degree helpless in the face of parental aggression, a helplessness increased by the structure of the modern family, and they are in practice, if not in theory, pretty much the possessions of the parents.

With more normal families a child elicits parental protection, care, and concern. The helplessness of a child is no more than a normal period of dependence upon the strength of parents who care for his needs and find happiness in doing so. For the abusing parents weakness elicits exploitation; possession is not a responsibility but a consolidation of power. If what these parents are seeking is victims rather than children, then their attitude is not so surprising; the psychology of people who seek victims is unfortunately familiar in many areas of life.

It would be good to think that abusing parents are rare, but unfortunately this may not be true. The recent report of the Children's Division of the American Humane Association on the incidence of child abuse found there were 662 cases reported in newspapers from January through December of 1962. They came from all but two of the fifty states. These 662 children came from 557 families. While they ranged in age from infancy through seventeen years, barely 10 percent of them were over ten years of age. The majority of the children, over 55 percent, were under four years of age. Of the 662 children, one in every four, or a total of 178, died as a result of parent-inflicted injuries. Over 80 percent of those killed were children under four.

The same report noted that fathers were responsible for 38 percent of the injuries and for 22 percent of the fatalities. Mothers had inflicted 28 percent of the injuries and 48 percent of the deaths. In 5 percent of the cases both parents had injured the children and in 5 percent both were responsible for the death of the children. Three out of four of the children killed had died at the hands of one or both parents. Step-parents, relatives, boy friends of the mother constituted a small percentage of those responsible.

The newspaper stories described children beaten with ... bare fists, straps, electric cords, T.V. aerials, ropes, rubber hose, fan belts, sticks, wooden spoons, pool cues, bottles, broom handles, baseball bats, chair legs and, in one case, a sculling oar. Less imaginative, but equally effective, was plain kicking with street shoes or with heavy work shoes.

Children had their extremities—hands, arms and feet—burned in open flames as from gas burners or cigarette lighters. Others bore burn wounds inflicted on their bodies with lighted cigarettes, electric irons or hot pokers. Still others were scalded by hot liquids thrown over them or from being dipped into containers of hot liquids.

Some children were strangled or suffocated by pillows held over their mouths or plastic bags thrown over their heads. A number were drowned in bathtubs and one child was buried alive.

To complete the list—children were stabbed, bitten, shot, subjected to electric shock, were thrown violently to the floor or against a wall, were stamped on and one child had pepper forced down his throat.

TYPES OF INJURIES

What kinds of injuries were inflicted on them?

The majority had various shapes, sizes and forms of bruises and contusions. There was a collection of welts, swollen limbs, split lips, black eyes and lost teeth. One child lost an eye.

Broken bones were common. Some were simple fractures; others compound. There were many broken arms, broken legs and fractured ribs. Many children had more than one fracture. One five month old child was found to have 30 broken bones in his little body.

The grimmest recital of all is the listing of internal injuries and head injuries. The head injuries particularly were a sizeable group. Both the internal injuries and the head injuries were responsible for a great many of the fatalities. In this group we find damage to internal organs such as ruptured livers, ruptured spleens and ruptured lungs. Injuries to the head were concussions or skull fractures, with brain hemorrhage and brain damage a frequent diagnosis.

This is indeed a grim, sad, sordid and horror-filled recital of what happens to children in communities in almost every state of the Union. It is made all the more so by the fact that this represents a compilation of specific situations—a cumulative report of the findings in 662 different cases[1].

---

[1]Children's Division, The American Humane Association Publication. Protecting the Battered Child (Denver, Colorado, 1962).

The recent study of Dr. Kempe[1] which undertook a nation-wide survey of hospitals for a period of one year, found that there were 302 reported cases of children under the age of three who had been severely injured by parents. Of this number, thirty-three died and eighty-five suffered permanent brain injury. When seventy-seven district attorneys were surveyed in like manner, they reported in a one-year span 477 cases of children under three. Of these, forty-five died and twenty-nine suffered permanent brain damage. Legal action followed one-third of the hospital cases and was initiated in 46 percent of the district attorney group. Dr. Kempe reports that in one day in November, 1961 four infants were brought to Colorado General Hospital with parent-inflicted injury. Two died in the hospital and a third died four weeks later after his return to parental care. The report of the American Medical Association, July, 1962, stated of child deaths from parental beatings, "It is likely that it will be found to be a more frequent cause of death than such well recognized and thoroughly studied diseases as leukemia, cystic fibrosis and muscular dystrophy, and it may well rank with automobile accidents."

Doctors call these small tragic victims "the battered children." The report of a study by Dr. Adelson of Cleveland was appropriately titled "Slaughter of the Innocents."[2] Dr. Adelson studied the files of the Cuyahoga County coroner's office and found forty-six homicides in which the victims were children. Over a period of seventeen years this was 3 percent of all the murders in the county. Thirty-seven of the forty-six children had been killed by parents or by persons in loco parentis. Ten of the children were babies under one year of age, eleven were aged one to three years, nine were between three and six years, eight were between six and ten, and eight were between eight and ten years of age or older.

[1]C. Henry Kempe, M.D., Denver; Frederic N. Silverman, M.D., Cincinnati; Brandt F. Steele, M.D., William Droegemueller, M.D., and Henry K. Silver, M.D., Denver, "The Battered Child Syndrome," Journal of the American Medical Association, July 7, 1962, Vol. 181, pp. 17–24.

[2]Lester Adelson, M.D., Cleveland, Ohio, "Slaughter of the Innocents— A Study of Forty-Six Homicides in Which the Victims Were Children," New England Journal of Medicine, June 29, 1961, Vol. 264; pp. 1345–1349.

Noting that "failure or inability to perform autopsies on infants found dead (or said to have been found dead) . . . will inevitably result in the missing of many cases of this type of homicide." Dr. Adelson observes that "Practically all the assaults resulting in these obscure homicides occurred in the home, where there were no environmental disturbances to indicate that fatal violence had been operative. It is relatively simple to destroy the life of a child in almost absolute secrecy without the necessity of taking any elaborate precautions to ensure that secrecy." He cites the case of a six-year-old girl who died a few moments after reaching the hospital. She had been living with an aunt and uncle and her seven year old sister. They reported that she had fallen from a swing the previous day. Post-mortem examination revealed "multiple contusions and abrasions of the head, trunk and extremities and healing burns of the genitalia and buttocks." In other words, the child had been tortured to death. The aunt and uncle were convicted of manslaughter.

It is a grim and terrifying story that emerges from the shadows of silence and denial. No one knows how many stricken children live day after day in suffering and fear unknown to any official agency. Some estimates run into the thousands. It is certain that the number far exceeds those now reported.

V : Profile of Abuse

Seventy-seven families out of the one hundred and eighty in the second section of the study abused their children; 24 percent did so severely and 20 percent moderately. In the first section of the study 90 of the 120 families abused their children, although no attempt was made in this exploratory part to determine degree. Why did the percentage of abusive families—75 percent in the first sampling and 44 percent in the second—differ so greatly? This is a puzzling question.

The cases in both samples were selected by the same criteria and in the same way. The specific items in the schedule applied to the second sample were drawn from the material abstracted from the first sample. The one clear differentiation was geography: all of the first 120 families were drawn from a large metropolitan area; only 40 of the second 180 families came from such a large urban center. There were no marked nationality or cultural differences between the two groups.

It may be that more child abuse occurs in the heavily populated areas. This certainly does not mean that the city itself causes parents to abuse their children. It may mean that the greater impersonality, the greater anonymity of the large city permits behavior like this to be more openly expressed. Perhaps also parental abuse may become more severe in a great city than in smaller cities and towns before it attracts community attention. The more severe cases of abuse in this study appeared in the large urban centers.

Parents, in this group of city dwellers, were brutal to their children. Their brutality overshadowed all other aspects of their behavior. While they had been classified in the first place by their frequent and violent beatings of their children, the results of the study demonstrated the consistency and extent of their cruelty. They assaulted their children; they beat them with ironing cords, wires, sticks, even pieces of lead pipe. Some parents kicked them, threw them violently across a room, slammed them into a wall. The scars and cuts on the children's bodies, the broken bones were mute witnesses of this brutality.

Physical torture was another aspect of brutality that could not be classified as beating. In its many forms it constitutes a horrifying picture: parents burned their children with lighted cigarettes, scalding water, hot stoves; parents knocked their children down with their fists; some parents bent back their child's fingers or twisted his arms, occasionally until the arm broke; other parents bit their children. Some form of physical torture appeared in 70 percent of the families in the severe abuse group.

The destruction of loved pets was another torture—not physical, but a torture nonetheless—indulged in by this group of parents. A dog or cat would suddenly disappear only to be discovered killed, or the animal would be killed in the child's presence. One father put his son's dog alive into a hot oven, forcing the boy to watch.

Abusive language and verbal expressions of hostility were common with more than 80 percent of the severely abusing families. Some parents stated bluntly that they hated their children and wished they were dead. Some threatened to kill them. Some remarked that they had never wanted them and it was a pity they had ever been born. Some parents yelled at children, calling them derogatory names and threatening them. Others said much the same things in quiet tones that were perhaps even more frightening. One father shaved his son's head and then called him "criminal." Others referred to their children as "idiots," "crazy," "monsters." Some emphasized to the child and to other people in the child's presence how ugly he was or how stupid or how hopelessly clumsy. Whatever the specific expression, they all conveyed the idea that the child was hopelessly inferior, an object of ridicule. Physical defects were mocked and any area in which a child was particularly sensitive or vulnerable was likely to be a special target for parental exploitation.

Children were consistently denied normal activities, prohibited the usual recreational and educational opportunities open to other children in the community at their economic level. School activities, sports, parties, neighborhood games, the clubs so dear to the heart of most children were forbidden to the children of many of these families. One young girl was finally, at the urging of her school teacher, permitted by her mother to attend a school dance. She came home glowing from perhaps the most carefree experience of her life. The next school dance she was promptly denied. In some families even neighborhood games and play were forbidden the children who often had to be home from school at a specific moment. Any delay—even so slight a one as that occasioned by a casual, impromptu bit of conversation—was dangerous to them. Opportunities to express individual interests, to satisfy curiosity normal for any child, to explore and pursue private projects usually a part of the learning experience of childhood were denied. In effect, the children were withdrawn from the contacts and experiences which might have taught them that not all families were like their own. The question, Why do abusing parents commonly do this? was not answered by the study. They might have been fearful of what their children would tell other people or perhaps this was merely another means of punishment—probably a bit of both motivated these parents. For the children the detachment was as disastrous for their future as for their present. Experiences with other children, the inevitable adaptations to any group of peers, the activities, games, and explorations are part of the preparation for adult living. From them the normal child gains confidence in himself. The isolation of the children in these families could only add to their frequent conviction that they were outsiders in this world, unable to partake of its warmth and vitality, alien and unwanted intruders.

There was an item in the schedule asking for any reasons the parents might have given for the punishments they inflicted.

The results are interesting. One of the most common responses was that the children wet and soil themselves. Since this is an almost inevitable reaction with children to extreme terror, the parents in effect punished them for what they themselves precipitated. What is normally conceived as toilet training, assistance to the young child in gradually developing his own self-control, would be impossible under circumstances that could only discourage such control. It is not surprising that many of the children in these families suffered from enuresis sometimes even into adolescence.

Another common reason for punishment was that the children drive the parents "crazy." While this is a common enough expression in any group and is probably upon occasion a universal parental reaction, it has obviously a very different meaning with abusing parents. Precisely what they do mean, what the children do or what it is about the children that precipitates this response, is not stated. The normal parent says, "If those children don't stop yelling they'll drive me crazy." These parents say only "They drive me crazy" without relation to any specific behavior. Other reasons scattered through the data are just as vague: "they are evil," "they are freaks," "they don't obey." Specific illustrations of what kind of behavior they are referring to in these pronouncements about their children are absent. The blanket statement is seemingly sufficient. When reasons are more specific, they tend to be bizarre: one father, for example, drew a chalk line on the floor and beat the children if they stepped over it.

In most cases parental explanations were not spontaneous. They tended to be reactions to the attitude of outsiders if not to their specific inquiries. In the absence of criticism, implicit or explicit, they rarely offered any explanations, and it is probable that they felt little need for such justification. They often had a bizarre quality in their reactions to other people as if they were not concerned with the same values and standards.

Human responses follow certain normal expectations and have an order and logic necessary for human communication. If one smiles at a friend, the usual expectation is that he will smile in return. If he does not, this raises a question of why he did not—his response was unexpected. He may have been absorbed in his own thoughts and unaware of the friendly smile, he may have been troubled about a problem of his own and not have felt like smiling, he may have been angry. The possibilities are numerous, but they demonstrate both the need for an explanation and the connected relation of that explanation. If the friend does not return the smile because a stranger in another part of town has a headache, this makes no sense to anyone; logic impels us to seek some connection, however obscure, between the two events. It is precisely this lack of connection that characterizes the bizarre responses of abusing parents.

A child is playing outside and the mother sits in the house talking to a visitor. They are discussing random subjects when abruptly the mother calls the child in and strikes her violently in the face. The immediate supposition is that the child was doing something to which the mother objected. The defect in this supposition is that the mother could not see the child, heard nothing, and gave no indication that she even suspected the child was doing anything objectionable. The blow had no overt connection with anything preceding it. A father knocks a child down and when he is asked the reason, replies that the child was washing a milk bottle. What is wrong with that seemingly innocuous occupation is never explained by the father. A mother holds her small child's hand on a hot stove until it is severely burnt to teach her to stay away from the stove so that she will not be burnt.

These bizarre responses do not mean that there is no cause for the actions. They are responses that violate normal, orderly expectations; their connections with the precipitating stimuli are obscure and tortuous. They spring from perceptions and motivations, inappropriate to the immediate reality. The fact that these disjointed responses play so important a part in the personal relationships of the severely abusing parents represents a significant clue to the quality of those relationships. It is hard to imagine anything more conducive to anxiety and fear in children than this confused, disorderly behavior.

This may explain why, with all the punishment inflicted by

these parents upon their children, they failed to provide any true discipline for them. There was too little consistent connection between what a child did and what he was punished for. What was expected of him at any given moment depended upon the mood of the parent. One day a five-minute delay in getting home from school could mean a beating; another day such a delay might elicit only indifference. Thus promptness itself was robbed of all meaning. Only the parent's unpredictable reaction mattered. A child could not learn the value of reliability and promptness when his total concentration was and could only be the avoidance of punishment.

Most of these children seem to settle finally for a blanket conviction that they are "bad," not bad for any reason, just bad. It is about the only conviction that can explain what happens to them, and it is one which often hardens into a life-time belief. What kind of self-image can a nine year old boy have who was told by his father that his mother attempted suicide because her small son was "so bad"? The answer is already visible in his behavior. He came to a Christmas party given by the agency working with this family. He stood in the crowd of excited children staring wistfully at the table loaded with cookies and Christmas candy. He did not dare to touch so much as a cookie until someone took him by the hand and told him, "They are for you too." At the age of nine he stands indicted as an attempted murderer of his own mother.

Unlike neglecting parents, those who abuse their children tend to be possessive of them. They refuse outside offers of help for their children, and they oppose friendships and personal attachments between persons outside the family and the children. An agency tried to lighten the burden of loneliness and fear for one boy by sending a young man to act as a kind of big brother to him, to take him to a ballgame, to visit a zoo, to enjoy the spring sunshine. The boy's mother allowed him to go twice, and each time she questioned him on his return. What did he say? What did the young caseworker say to him? After the second time she refused to let the boy go again. The child had said nothing in criticism of his mother, but he was growing fond of the caseworker. In a way that boy was worse off than before. He had tasted a little normal living, and then he had been abruptly cut off from it.

This kind of behavior was true of 59 percent of the severely abusing families. These were the parents who denied their children needed help, whether it was educational, medical, or recreational. They were noticeably secretive and did not like to have people talk to their children when they were not present. Their suspicious attitude implied that any offers of help for the children were an excuse to indict them.

This suspiciousness seemed to be common among parents like these. One perceptive caseworker noticed that almost invariably they kept the doors of their houses locked and their window shades drawn. It was often necessary for a caseworker to go through more than one closed door before reaching the family. Neglecting families, on the other hand, rarely locked their doors in the daytime—the doors might open on chaos, but everything was visible.

Some abusing families in this study also neglected their children. They did not feed them adequately, did not keep them clean or dress them properly. Abusing parents were more apt to keep their houses and children clean than they were to feed the children adequately. There were families who kept their houses and their children immaculately clean, followed a daily routine, and fed their children well enough. When child abuse occurs in middle-class families, the parents usually do not neglect physical care of their children—not, at least, in ways visible to the outside community.

Three quarters of the severely abusing families failed, however, to secure medical care for their children. Since medical treatment is vital to future as well as present physical well-being and may be essential to life itself, the parental lack of care in this area was particularly destructive to the children. In some families it was clearly intentional rather than the result of indifference. Even when a social agency wished to provide such care, the parents refused permission. In one case a two year old child lay in his crib with a broken leg for several days before the parents finally brought him to the hospital for care. Illness was often ignored, and a baby brought to the hospital

severely ill with pneumonia had by parental admission been
burning with fever for days.

There was a tendency to ridicule the importance of physical
injuries or illness in children. It was, in fact, a way of saying
that their lives were not very important. Since the injuries
were in many cases parent-inflicted, this was a further emphasis of the precariousness of life itself for these children. While
children from severely neglecting homes were also health en-
dangered, they were at least spared inflicted injuries and the
menace of intended deprivation.

Despite their open expression of hatred for their children
most of these parents objected to their removal from the home.
Sometimes they said openly that placement of the children
would be a reflection on them; sometimes they were angry at
the intrusion and declared that they could do what they liked
with their own children. Only when the situation became too
threatening to them, when the children were the source of too
much trouble for them, were they more willing to agree to their
placement out of the home. When only a single child in the
family was abused, some of the parents were passively agree-
able to his removal. There were seven of these families with a
"scapegoat" child in this study. When they agreed to placement,
they were usually willing to give up that child permanently.

Few of the abusing parents left their children alone at home.
It would have been unusual, for instance, for them to leave a
baby alone for hours. In fact, some of the abusive mothers rarely
left the house. They sat at home with a grim tenacity that rejected the normal interests and activities of life. Yet in other
ways they were totally irresponsible. The children's behavior was
likely to be ignored unless it brought unpleasant repercussions
to the parents, and sometimes even then it elicited little more
than indifference. Withdrawn, fearful behavior was ignored or
ridiculed. Aggressive behavior aroused little concern so long as
it was directed toward people and things of no interest to the
parents: one child precipitated school alarm by his wanton torturing of a cat; another child abruptly and for no discernible
reason threw a stone at a stranger on the street. In both cases
the parents were passively indifferent.

The moderate abuse group of families was similar to the severe abuse type, but parental behavior was less extreme. While 25 percent of this group practiced some kind of physical torture, this was both less severe in degree and less common in occurrence. A father's knocking a child down or slamming him against a wall is violent and destructive behavior but can be labeled moderate abuse when it happens only once or twice. It lacks the deadly continuity and the refinement of cruelty. These parents were less likely to deny normal activities and recreation to their children, less likely to deny them help or outside friendships. They were often abusive in their language, but 58 percent of them made some statements favorable to their children, expressing something positive in their relationship. They were a long way from ideal parents, but they were notably more moderate in their behavior than the parents in the severe abuse group.

The moderate and severe abuse groups come together, however, in the parents' relationship to each other. It was found that one parent commonly dominated the other—a dominance based on fear, not the strength of responsibility—often to an extreme degree. The parent who abused the children also abused his marital partner. Sometimes that abuse was physical, more often it took a less gross but even more deadly form. For example, one man concentrated on his wife's supposed infidelity to the point where he woke her in the middle of the night to tell her that he had discovered she had a lover. His wife's frantic denials were received with cold scorn. With time the wife began to wonder if she had spells of amnesia when she did not know what she was doing—perhaps her husband was right, and she did not remember. She clung to him even when he told her that she was unfit to share his home. When she told him that she loved him, he laughed and told her to prove it by killing herself. One day she tried to do just that.

In the hospital she sent for the caseworker who had been trying to help the family. Her first words were, "Take my children. Don't leave them there." Later she told the caseworker, "I've been so confused. I didn't know whether my husband was right. You see I've thought of him as God, and anything he said must be right. Now I don't know. I thought I loved him, but I think he is for me like an addiction." Nothing describes better this strange relationship where one is the self-imposed prisoner of the other. Caught in this morbid struggle the prisoner-parent can do little to protect the children.

Following in this irresponsible, destructive course, it is not surprising that the abusive partner takes little if any responsibility for his actions. He or she makes the decisions and gives the orders, but will not take responsibility for their consequences. Like dictatorial children, they do as they please and leave someone else to clear away the wreckage. Their power is well-nigh absolute within the limited domain of the family.

Many of the caseworkers who saw these families assumed that the parents would feel guilty about their actions. If this was so, there was no evidence of it in the records. The abusive parent behaved as if he saw nothing wrong in what he did and the passive parent, absorbed in his own wrongs, seemed oblivious to his own responsibility in the situation. Ninety-five percent of the parents continued to treat their children abusively despite agency intervention and outside criticism. Some of them when they asked the court for the return of their child, said they were sorry for their behavior and promised to change it. Subsequent reports showed no change.

Ninety percent of the parents indicated no spontaneous expression of regret; on the contrary, they seemed to see no need for such a reaction. When they were criticized, they blamed other people, often the children, accusing them of the behavior that was in fact their own. More than one parent said angrily that there was nothing else he could do when the children were so "bad," but there were no specifics about what the children had done. There was only the blanket indictment of "badness." More than any other group the severe abuse families blamed others. Often the children in desperation blamed themselves.

As a group the abusive parents seemed to see other people as victims, resources, or enemies. They made contacts rather than friends. They trusted no one. They did not often visit other people, and they invited few into their houses. They rarely joined groups or organizations and most of them did not participate in religious groups. As they frightened others, so they themselves responded chiefly to fear.

VI : The Social Setting

What about the economic and social levels of these families? How much money did they have to spend, what kind of houses and neighborhoods did they live in, what were their education and employment, and what were their health problems and social ills?

Most of the families studied were poor, many of them very poor. Out of the 300 families in the total sample, 128 had at one time or another been given public assistance. In the second study, 78 of the 95 cases where income was recorded were living on $400 a month or less. Of all 180 families in the second study, only 20 percent had less than three children at the time the records were read, and 37 percent had between six and twelve children. Out of the 300 families only 32 were financially comfortable and able to meet their physical needs.

In general, housing was also poor. The study took as a standard of adequacy in housing that space would approximate roughly one room to a person, and that there would be modern plumbing and lighting—by that standard only 64 families of the 300 lived under adequate conditions. For most of the others the chronic problems of overcrowding, poor repair, lack of modern conveniences were everywhere present. Poorly heated, vermin-ridden, in various states of disrepair, much of the housing was a hazard to health.

Equally hazardous to these families was the sporadic employment. In 58 percent of the families the wage earner, usually the father, had not held one job continuously for as long as two years. In 71 percent of the families the wage earner was an unskilled laborer. Most of the parents had limited education, and the general average was grammar school or less.

When these facts are put together, there emerges the familiar picture of poverty, poor housing, unemployment, large numbers of children. It would be easy to assume that neglect and abuse of children is an outcome of this economic picture or is a more or less natural accompaniment of it, but it would be easy to be wrong about this. Our sample was selected largely from public child welfare which tends to get a heavy concentration of families that are economically deprived. Yet even in this sample, 19 percent of the families belonged to the middle class, assuming that skilled workers, men in business, and white collar workers are to be termed middle class. Further, there is no evidence that low income families as such neglect or abuse their children. On the contrary, such studies as that of ADC in Chicago would indicate that this is not true. If a family lacks the money to buy the amount of milk, fresh fruit, meat that children need for good nutrition or to give them the kind and amount of clothing that more prosperous children have, this does not constitute parental neglect. It is parental misfortune. When the parents do the best they can with what they have, the children may be poor but they are not neglected. In this study, the children were both poor and neglected.

Of the 300 families, 237 were white, 54 were Negro, and 9 were either Indian or Oriental. In five of the ten localities used in the total research sample there was a considerable Negro population. In this study there was no correlation with race or nationality. The survey of the American Humane Society on the incidence of abuse noted also that most of the parents were native born and no nationality, cultural, or religious group predominated.

Reports on family health were not complete and lacked standardized categories, but they were sufficient to show that over half of the families had serious health problems. Chronic and acute illnesses were common and medical care was minimal since the families sought medical care only in emergencies. Sixteen percent of the children had been hospitalized or medically treated for severe malnutrition and dehydration.

This did not include the much larger number who were undernourished and suffered health problems resulting therefrom. Both parents and children suffered an interminable succession of infections. In the 180 families of the second study 41 percent of the mothers and 31 percent of the children suffered major health problems. The fathers were relatively healthy—only 22 percent had major health complaints.

One of the most acute problems was alcoholism. One hundred and eighty-six parents were severe and chronic drinkers and their drinking constituted a primary family problem. While many other parents drank heavily, they were not included in this number since drinking was not the primary problem. The mother who spent her nights and sometimes her days in cheap taverns, the father who gave most of his paycheck to the local bar could do little else but neglect their children. In some of the families there was a history of alcoholism going through three generations.

Along with alcoholism and heavy drinking went a whole barrage of social and psychological problems. One hundred and six parents were diagnosed psychotic, and this figure almost certainly errs on the low side. For many families no psychiatric study or consultation was available. One hundred and twelve parents, not including the much larger number arrested for drunkenness, desertion, disturbance of the peace, had a record of at least one crime. In most cases this was petty theft or some form of minor crime but occasionally included more serious charges. There were three murderers. Promiscuity was common although not as major a problem as might have been supposed. Eighty-two parents were consistently promiscuous. Mental retardation was probably widespread but this cannot be proved because so few of the parents had received psychological examinations; of the 110 who had, 58 were mentally retarded.

While the record on the parents is incomplete, it is even sketchier for their children. Of the 890 children, 8 percent had been adjudged delinquent. This figure does not include truancy and 41 percent of the school age children were truants. While the accuracy of these figures is hedged by lack of complete reporting, it is probable that they are an underestimation of the extent of delinquency rather than the reverse. The children in these families show indications of a high proportion of minor delinquencies but a low proportion of crimes of violence and those requiring organized planning. They may steal when the opportunity occurs, but they are less likely to be the organizers of a series of thefts. They tend to be followers rather than initiators.

So few of them have had psychiatric and psychological examinations that no estimate can be made of the number of psychotic and mentally retarded children there are in these families. Of the 890 children in the second study, 13 had been diagnosed as psychotic and 54 as mentally retarded. There can be small question that the actual number is considerably higher.

Even allowing for the fact that none of these problems are mutually exclusive and that one parent and one family may show all or most of them the figures add up nevertheless to a horrifying degree of pathology. They trace the outline of a family life that upon the shifting sands of economic deprivation grows physical, social, and emotional illness. These are disintegrating families. What, then, happens to marriages in these families? Surprisingly, of the 300 families, 196 were parents married and living together, 104 were one-parent homes, 30 were unmarried mothers, 70 were divorced, deserted or separated, and in 4, one parent was dead. Unfortunately this picture is rather misleading. Divorces were common in this group as the marital history of the parents revealed. Thirty-eight percent of the parents had had at least one divorce (as contrasted with the national average of roughly 24 percent) and some of them had divorced and remarried three and four times. The fact that they usually remarried quickly accounts for the large number married and living together at the time of the case reading. Frequently some of the children belonged to one parent and some to both, making it impossible to differentiate on the basis of those children who had already lived through a broken marriage.

Much more common than divorce were the temporary separations. These could not practicably be counted since they varied from a few days to a few months. They were a frequent solution to parental quarrels, family crises, and such recurring difficulties as eviction from house or apartment. The father faced with financial crisis and family quarrels solved his dilemma for the moment by leaving for a matter of days or weeks. In effect this was a temporary desertion until hopefully the crisis should have been weathered. In other cases a particularly violent fight might precipitate the departure of one of the parents for as long as a year. Or a harassed wife might tell her alcoholic husband to leave. More often than not he moved nearby, continued to visit the family at will, and moved back when her mood had softened or she had resigned herself to the inevitable. Sometimes these separations and returns continued over years.

Despite the misery of these marriages and the disorganization of the parents' lives a surprising number continued to stay together. This cannot be construed to mean, as the records made sharply clear, that they ever made a good home or a productive marriage. They simply stayed together. With some, of course, there was a succession of marital partners, legal and otherwise. The reason parents stayed together did not lie in their devotion to each other nor did tradition or convention impell them.

Probably part of the answer lay with their general apathy. Change on a planned level requires energy, and many of these parents were drifters who were pushed by the pressure and energy of outside events but did not themselves push against those events. When they separated, it was an impulsive action, a seeking of temporary escape from which they returned in much the same way as they had left. Beyond this and probably more imperative was their need of each other. It is easy to forget that there are destructive needs whose fulfillment brings misery, not contentment, and that these needs can be quite as demanding and much more insatiable than those which feed life. The needs whose fulfillment integrates and opens new sources of vitality are healthy needs. The needs of these parents sought fulfillment in destruction of themselves and each other, but they were no less needs because of that.

Some of the unhappiest marriages in this study were ones where the parents had never been separated. They seemed to live on the destructiveness they created for themselves and each other; their mutual exploitation created a bond between them of amazing endurance. The fact of this strange bond, however, was no index to the unity of the family or the health of the marriage.

In their economic and social framework, then, these families are chiefly members of the lower economic group, limited in education, unskilled in occupation, given to frequent changes of jobs and periods of unemployment. They live to a considerable extent in substandard housing, overcrowded, dirty, in poor repair. When they live in the cities, they tend to congregate in the slums. They have large numbers of children with few material resources for their care. They may be white or Negro, Catholic or Protestant, of any nationality group. They are burdened with health problems, major and minor, and they have little medical care. Many of them are alcoholics, more are heavy drinkers. Some of them are psychotic, probably many more than are officially diagnosed, and some of them are mentally retarded, probably many more than are officially listed. Many of them are known to the police for petty crimes and misdemeanors, and a few of them commit serious crimes. Some are promiscuous and some make and break a series of marriages, yet many do continue to stick to their marriages. Most of them were married and living together at the time of this study although this was often not the first marriage for either partner.

This description does not mean that parents who neglect or abuse their children are necessarily all like this. It describes most of the parents in this study, but there were middle-class families even in this sample. There is nothing here to substantiate an assumption that neglect and abuse of children are confined solely to this group and this economic and social class.

VII : Why Does It Happen?

What causes the existence of abusive and neglectful parents?
Why do people behave like this and how does it start? The
suffering of children, the misery of parents, the untold loss to
our society are accompaniments of their existence. Even without exact knowledge of their numbers it is clear that they form
a group heavy with suffering and failure and costly to the fine
balances of modern life. Surely this miserable existence was
not chosen by them.

No one really knows the cause. There has been no thorough
study of their life histories. There are theories and speculations
and it is likely that there are multiple reasons for the existence
of such grim behavior. Probably the most common assumption
is that such parents are the creations of their environment. If
children grow up in homes like these, they will in turn create
the same kind of homes for their children. While this study was
not designed to explore causation, it did note the family background of parents when such information was available in the
records. On a good number there was no information at all. Yet
there was enough to offer some clues.

There was at least some recording of background for 301
fathers and mothers. One hundred and fifty-eight of them had
come from homes where they were physically neglected or
abused, homes exactly like their current ones. More of them
seemed to come from neglecting than abusing homes but this
may be more the result of lack of sufficient information than
of the actual situation. The vignettes of their past, their own
spontaneous comments about it, picture parents who never

themselves had a childhood. In fact, it is hard with many of
them to see how they could have been different than they are
in the light of their own family experience.

Jane Neilson, white, of no known religion, was the oldest
of ten children. Her mother was promiscuous and her father
alcoholic. The children were all left to care for themselves, and
they were familiar with hunger, filth, cold, and confusion. The
mother encouraged the daughters to become prostitutes and
took part of their earnings. Jane and three of her sisters were
arrested as sex delinquents. Jane went to the state correctional
school at age fifteen because she had been prostituting herself
with a man in his fifties. Two brothers were arrested for stealing. One boy had severe chronic asthma and was receiving
no medical care. The three younger children were finally removed from the home as a consequence of severe physical
neglect.

Subsequently, Jane had six children, two of them illegitimate.
She finally married a man with a criminal record who was
abusive to her and the children. There were frequent separations, and her husband was again arrested, this time for larceny.
Jane drank heavily and drifted from crisis to crisis. Three of the
children were removed and are under the care of agencies. At
the time the record was read there were complaints of the
neglect of the other three and a request pending with the court
for their removal. This woman's entire life had been dreary
misery, a saga of exploitation, deprivation, indifference and
hate. What she could have given any child is hard to see.

Sixty-six parents seemed to have been severely rejected by
their families, but there was no clear indication of physical
neglect or abuse. While too little is known about what happened to them, they themselves were convinced that they had
been unwanted in their own homes. Some of the grandparents
were described as domineering and others as both dominating
and indulgent. One neglecting mother described her childhood
as an endless search for a home. Her parents were divorced
when she was small, and each remarried. She went from one to
another, an unwanted obligation to each. Her mother preferred
her sister and made this fact abundantly clear to her. She

describes her mother as domineering and indifferent to her interests.

One interestingly verifying incident occurred in this situation. The caseworker working with the mother and her family talked with the maternal grandmother. For some reason the caseworker remarked that the mother and the grandmother were much alike. The mother was openly pleased and the grandmother was just as openly displeased. The grandmother gave no help to this family and seemed to ignore its existence.

Forty-five parents grew up in institutions or foster homes. Little is recorded about these placements, some of which were made by the grandparents directly. One father had been deserted by both his parents, placed in an institution at age four and never saw either parent again. It is doubtful that these placements were happy ones.

Twenty-three parents were described as different in behavior from the other members of their families. A number of them came from middle-class homes where there was no evidence of economic deprivation. Several of them indicated that they felt themselves to be the rejected ones of the family, regarded by the others as the failure. One woman observed that she had always been the "dumb" one in her family. Others had parents who themselves remarked that this child had always been a problem. Brothers and sisters were described as successful and stable; in the few instances where the siblings were interviewed, they seemed reluctant to talk about or to have anything to do with their relative. In fact, consistently, the grandparents and other members of the family had almost no contact with this "black sheep" and his family and took little responsibility for protecting the grandchildren. While much more information about them is necessary, it appears that for some reason this one child was set apart from the rest of the family and regarded as more of a technical than emotional member of it.

Of the 301 parents only nine seemed to have had any positive relationship with a member of their own family, either with a parent, or with a relative. These were the only ones who talked about memories of their own childhoods with any pleasure.

Sketchy as all this information is it lends evidence to the assumption that childhood environment played a big role in the causation of the pathological families described here. Many of them never knew anything different.

Neglect in particular may have been caused by childhood environment in combination with economic and social circumstances. The cause of abuse however, is not so clear. Among those in this study some abusing parents had come from neglecting homes, and some of the neglecting parents had themselves been abused as children. There is no evidence yet that any great proportion of abusing parents have themselves been abused as children. Behavior so extreme and so bizarre as parental abuse of children might well not be explainable in any simple or ordinary terms.

A number of psychiatrists believe that there is an organic or constitutional factor involved. In other words, for some unknown reason some people are born with a predisposition toward this kind of personality. Environment may deter or encourage its development, but its seeds are already present in the person. This would certainly help to explain that gap in communication so often experienced with abusive parents, as if they acted on different premises than other people.

The complexity of this problem is well illustrated by two boys, ages ten and eleven, who were living in a children's institution. Both had been removed from their homes because they had been badly abused by their fathers. One father had wrapped newspapers around his small son's arm and set them afire. The other father had burned his son with lighted cigarettes and beaten him with wire. In both families the mothers were passive, detached, afraid. Both boys had been placed in the same institution for relatively the same length of time.

Yet these two were startlingly different. One was cold, often cruel, with no interest in any other person. He could be charming toward adults from whom he wanted something and forget them when they were of no further use to him. He enjoyed hurting other children but rarely had any open fights with them. He slammed a door on one child cutting his head and afterward could see no reason why adults were so upset since he "had only cut him a little." Why he had done it was a question he could not or would not answer. He had no friends, never talked about himself or his past life. There was a strangely unchildlike quality about him.

His difference from the other children was sharply etched by his response to an accident in which another child cut his hand badly. The child was crying with pain, and the hand was bleeding profusely. Some of the children around him ran for help, others tried to stop the bleeding while others hid their faces from the sight. Only this one boy pushed through the circle of youngsters and stared with open pleasure at the bleeding child. He seemed unaware or indifferent to the involuntary movement of the others away from him. They were afraid of him.

The second of the two boys was pale, undersized, reticent. He did not often oppose anyone, child or adult; he was easily exploited and pushed around by other children unless adults intervened. He made little attempt to ingratiate himself, and he kept his fears and nightmares to himself. Yet when someone reached out to him, showed concern for him, he could respond with a shy pleasure. He had interests, liked to talk about things he read and learned in school. He could have cruel impulses, to tease and frighten a younger child, but they were evanescent, mild in expression, without violence or calculation. He did not make strong friendships, but he had some friends and was generally liked by other children. He was often sick, had minor accidents, was easily hurt.

These two boys had both been subjected to horrible aggression, and both had to live with hate and violence within themselves. One turned it upon other people and met the world with cold ferocity. The other turned it upon himself and seemed to be consuming his own life. Why these two with backgrounds seemingly so similar were at this young age so deeply different is an unanswerable question at this stage in our knowledge. It is true that there is much about them that we do not know—there may have been experiences of great impact which appear in no official record. It is also true that they began life with different endowments, endowments that may have been the determining factor in how they reacted to the bitter experiences of their lives. If we could answer the question of why these two boys are so different, we would have taken a long step in the direction of learning what causes human problems such as these.

One question that inevitably arises is what role social level plays in all this. Do these families behave like this because they are lower class? Or are they low in the income scale because they behave like this—without goals, organization, or stability? That most of the families in this study belong to the lower economic group, is no surprise since the sample was drawn largely from public agencies. Other studies such as the St. Paul Family Centered Project[1] have, however, shown a clear correlation between family disorganization and social class. The more extensive the disorganization the more likely it is that the family will belong to the lower economic group. While this clearly establishes a relationship between the two, it does not define in what way class is a causative factor in family disorganization. There are a number of questions and problems inherent in the conclusion that class explains the kind of families in this study.

For example, many lower class families do not conform to these behavioral patterns. Economic limitations can and do exist without accompanying family disintegration. The findings of a recent study by Willie[2] in comparing "problem" and "stable" families in a lower income population showed definitive differences between the two in the structure and composition of the households. He notes that "the haste with which problem families marry, have children, separate, and then have more children suggests that their behavior is uncontrolled and that they are uncommitted." He did not find this pattern typical

[1]Geismar, Ludwig L. and Beverly Ayres. Families in Trouble—An Analysis of the basic social characteristics of 100 families served by the project, (St. Paul: Family Centered Project, 1958).

[2]Willie, Charles V. "The Structure and Composition of 'Problem' and 'Stable' Families in a Lower Income Population" (unpublished paper based on findings of Ford Foundation Project at Syracuse University Youth Development Center, 1961).

for the stable group of families. He suggests that "the behavior of problem families is deviant from and in opposition to human social organization. They are not conforming to a sub-cultural group."

The study of ADC families[1] in Chicago brought out the same results. The profile of family disorganization was not a carbon copy for the lower economic group. The report observed, "The public has gained a false image of a mother who is shiftless and lazy, unwilling to work, promiscuous and neglectful of her children . . . . This study found very few mothers, not more than 3 percent, who fit this image in one or more ways."

Class, per se cannot explain why there are families like these. It can, however, define the circumstances in which they could develop. Social class, by the behavioral standards it imposes and enforces, permits or prohibits what the individual family acts out in plain view of the community. In other words, both society and the classes which compose it set a certain climate in which specific kinds of behavior may flourish or wither.

Thus, lack of economic resources tends to make deviant behavior more visible to the outside community. The request for financial assistance exposes a family to an investigation that would under other circumstances be summarily rejected as an invasion of privacy. The delinquent act of a child from a prosperous home may be shielded from official cognizance—the family might make financial restitution or might place the child in a private school. The delinquent act of a child from a lower income home is much more likely to attract official knowledge and action because the family lacks the resources for any alternative solution. In general, lower income families with low prestige and frequent ignorance of official methods and knowledge have less means of concealing deviant behavior. Obviously the more visible the behavior, the greater the likelihood that it will command community awareness and attention.

The question of visibility or invisibility is a very important one. It is easy to assume that unseen behavior does not exist

[1]"Facts, Fallacies and Future—Summary of a Study of the ADC Program in Cook County-Welfare Council of Metropolitan Chicago," 1962, Chicago, Ill.

simply because it is not seen. Further, social controls must of necessity confine themselves to behavior that can by some means be known to others. Only when the standards of a society are so thoroughly inculcated in its individual members that they are self-enforced does the question of invisibility become largely irrelevant. Much of the behavior of the families in this study had become visible, but only certain parts of that behavior would under other circumstances—such as would prevail in the middle class—be necessarily visible. Disorganization in interpersonal relationships is not necessarily visible. The sharing of interests, activities, and problems is not easily open to community observation nor does the lack of such sharing attract official intervention. Further, a family may be physically together and share little but space. Even behavior such as lack of consistent discipline of the children and parental fighting in the presence of the children might well remain concealed unless it resulted in behavior so extreme as to require police action. As a matter of fact, the complaints which brought the families in this study to official attention were not concerned with this behavior, and the behavior itself became visible only after agency study and intervention rendered such observations possible.

Although family disorganization in general cannot be confined to one class, physical neglect, at least in the extreme degree found in this study, seems to show a clear classconnection. The underfeeding of children, the dirt and deterioration of the households, the lack of family routine are all behaviors of high visibility to the community. Most of the complaints attracting attention to these families centered in these items. Any middle-class family sending children to school in such a state of physical neglect or feeding children so inadequately that they required hospitalization for malnutrition would be extremely conspicuous and heavily penalized within its own group. Social controls are specific and powerful in this area, and the wish and ability to conform to them constitutes in itself a considerably greater degree of family organization than that observable in the families in this sample.

It is, of course, possible that this kind of behavior can exist in a circumscribed degree and be relatively invisible. But the very limitation of degree implies a respect for and conformity to social control not found in the families in this study. It seems reasonable to assume that any family ignoring social controls in this area would rapidly be in serious trouble.

Punitiveness toward children is visible to the community roughly in proportion to the extent of physical severity. Cruel and derogatory words leave no visible marks, but broken bones, cuts, and bruises attract attention. A good bit of physical abuse can be concealed, of course, and marks resulting from severe beatings are not necessarily observable. The father who commented that he never left marks on the bodies of his children where they would show was well aware of this. Furthermore, even such physical injuries as broken bones are easily attributable to accident. While consistent and severe parental abuse of children is to some degree usually observable, it is ironically also concealed by higher social status.

With the families in this study observable abuse brought official intervention even where final proof was lacking. Had these families belonged to a middle-class group, even in the absence of any greater efforts at concealment, official agencies would have shown greater hesitation in taking action. In the absence of proof of parental abuse the family's economic and social status would tend to protect the abusing parent or parents from direct community action and to contribute to concealment of the behavior. Many of the children about whom doctors have become alarmed are from middle-class homes.

The establishment and maintenance of consistent standards of behavior for children is a factor that has both visible and invisible components. In the obvious and extreme form seen in these families lack of standards has a degree of visibility that is probably class-connected. Such expectations of children as regular attendance at school, progression in school work, conformity with minimum social controls, tend to be lacking, and their absence is easily observable to the outside community. Their absence would be more conspicuous in a middle-class family and would almost certainly result in social censure. Value standards relating to behavior not necessarily visible may, however, present a different picture.

While with the exception of gross physical neglect, none of these factors taken singly appear to show any necessary class-relationship, their existence in conjunction with each other—as in the behavioral profiles of these families—may well be so related. In other words, when this kind of disorganized behavior occurs in every area of living, there is small chance that a family would be middle-class or could remain so. A conspicuous distinction with these families is their seeming indifference to social control. The social pressures which in other groups compel at least minimum outward conformity have little effect upon the families in this study except as they are officially and specifically implemented. This has the effect of isolating them from any established class structure.

Most of the families in this study had little to lose—social status, economic security, community respect, the good opinion of other people were all lacking and for most of them always had been. They may have wished they had some or all of these advantages, but if so, their wishing was a wistful longing for the moon not a force compelling them to effort. They had no incentive to change their behavior nor to limit it—they feared no loss and expected no rewards. Social control had lost its major weapons and relinquished its place to official and legal controls.

This process has unquestionably been hastened and promoted by the rapidity of urbanization, the mobility of population, and the abandonment of whole sections of the city to families both rootless and economically deprived. The small town had its disorganized families, but there were sharp and firm limits to the family's behavior, at least so far as that behavior was known. In the slums of a modern city, no such personal controls are possible. The contacts are broken, the old sense of personal responsibility—a community accepting the obligation to do something about its own problems—is weakened. The physical distance of a few miles has become a human distance ocean wide.

In one small town a child of two years was tied out in the yard of his home in the broiling sun of a hot August day. There was no way he could reach any shade. Within an hour three different people had reported this to the sheriff. Driving by they had observed the child's plight and promptly taken action. They knew the child's family, they knew the sheriff, and they knew and shared the community's concern for the children. The youngster was out of the sun in an hour. In an urban area, people driving by might be disturbed by the sight of the baby in the sun, but they would be unlikely to know the family, know whom to call, and almost certainly would have no conviction of community support and approval. Individual responsibility becomes under these circumstances increasingly difficult to assume. It is easier to leave it to the "proper authorities."

In effect the lower class disorganized family has been isolated from the rest of society. There are no natural channels of communication between this group and those whose standards are violated by it. This does not mean that these families are a unified group outside of or against the major society. For that they would require standards of their own which they supported and to which they conformed, however different those standards might be from those accepted by the majority group; for that they would require an in-group feeling which bound them together, however antagonistic it might be to the society which excluded them. But these are families which belong to no organized group, which support no standards, state no values. They drift, caught up in forces they neither understand nor oppose. In their isolation they are more likely to tend toward disintegration than the organized effort of opposition.

Child neglect and child abuse are no integral part of any class culture, but the conditions of modern living, particularly of urban life, promote their grossness and very possibly their extent in the most economically deprived class. The behavior of the families is visible to official agencies but not to that part of the community which would otherwise set limits to it. The grossness and openness of their behavior must be to some extent the result of their social isolation. There is in a sense no one to hide from, no one even to notice until official action moves into the picture, and official action is remote, impersonal, alien. Only families with values internally accepted and internally enforced could maintain standards of behavior under these circumstances and such families do not often neglect or abuse their children.

It may well be that in our modern society family behavior becomes more hidden from those social forces that once set limits to it. Despite the picture window, open-patio living of the modern suburb there may be much less meaningful visibility of parental behavior than there was even fifty years ago. Mobility of population, concentration of numbers, separation of family members tend to break the continuity of personal knowledge and experience, to weaken the sense of personal responsibility. Behavior is observed in bits and pieces, often by different groups with little mutual contact. Consistency except in the employment area is not easily observed nor enforced. What is seen from the outside is frequently partial, transient, detached from the whole picture. Even if the neighbors are alarmed by things they see, they know that they or the family may move soon and it is better not to get involved. When people lived for three generations in the same community, there was not much they did not know about one another, and at least visible behavior was subject to social control. It certainly did not guarantee the protection of children, but it did set limits beyond which no family could step with impunity.

There is much that is not clear about what causes families like those in this study and much that is not known. Individual environment in combination with social environment is certainly one important element. Beyond that are crucial questions to which as yet there are no answers. What part does mental retardation play in the development of neglect and abuse patterns? Is it more frequent with these families than among families of more acceptable behavior? What about psychosis, particularly with abusing parents? Are most of them mentally ill and if so, what has caused that illness? Do the demands and pressures of our speeded-up society cause problems such as these, or does the society merely push the problems to the surface? Sooner or later we must find answers to these questions.

What about the children now growing up in these families? Will they in turn duplicate for their children the same dreary life of defeat and misery? There is a fair presumption that most of them will. The only way of life that they know intimately is the one they were born into, the one that they live now.

Observations of the children in the records show this grim cycle repeating itself. Most of them have already had serious problems. Some of them are aggressive, destructive, bitter, and suspicious. Others are apathetic, depressed, silent. Truancy, school failure, isolation from school groups are common. The most noticeable omission from the accounts of their lives is laughter and play. A deep layer of depression seems to underlie all their behavior. They seem to be without incentive, without hope, without the surging vitality that gives youth its bright promise.

Yet the most hopeful thing about them is the eagerness with which many of them reached out for something better, given the chance. When someone showed personal interest, the children responded, tentatively at first, but still reaching for a hope. The question that only our society can answer is: will there be a hope for them?

VIII : The Protectors

What happens when a complaint comes to the child welfare agency and a social worker is handed the job of doing something about it? What do you say when you knock on a door and a strange woman opens it and stares suspiciously at you? She didn't ask for you and she's not often cordial when you arrive.

Some caseworkers who in anxious desperation have said that they heard the family had "problems" and they were there to help have been met with more suspicion and frequently the bland answer, "No, we haven't got any problems." Since no argument on this line is possible, the caseworker must come to the flat truth that a complaint has been lodged about the parent's behavior. The wise caseworker begins with that fact and with the firm conviction that it is his job to find out what is happening to the children.

Many abusing families react angrily: "Who told you such lies?" When the caseworker refuses to say, the abusing parent may speculate about "who is trying to make trouble for me." But the first job for the caseworker is to concentrate on determining the facts, not on who made the complaint. Naturally the parents would prefer to discuss the latter, and the effective caseworker takes the initiative and tackles the real problem of what is happening to the children.

This is not a simple task—few abusive parents will admit under these circumstances that they have done anything other than discipline their children in normal fashion. Two things help the caseworker: one, observation of the family and household and, two, the defective reality judgment of the parents.

No amount of protestation by the parents can disguise the fear in these families, the frozen stillness of the children, the anxious corroboration of the passive parent to every belligerent statement of the aggressive partner. The children watch and listen with the wary tension of frightened animals. When a parent asserts "My children love me. They're always wanting to be with me. Isn't that true?" the children hastily proclaim their devotion, their words at variance with their anxious faces.

The parents in their determination to convince this official intruder of their impeccable behavior continue to expostulate on how well they treat their children. Here they begin to betray themselves, because seemingly they have little inner sense that there is anything wrong with what they do. Thus Mrs. Smith, stepmother to four children, explains that she used to beat the children before the school nurse told her it was wrong, but now she doesn't beat them so hard. When the caseworker asks how the children's arms have been burned, Mrs. Smith is suddenly blank. She doesn't know. Perhaps they were playing with matches outside. Her face is expressionless, and she shrugs her shoulders as if to dismiss an irrelevant subject.

The school had complained that the Smith children often showed marks of beating on their bodies, were fearful of talking to anyone, often slept in class as if they were exhausted. When the caseworker, Mrs. Rill, visited the home, she thought at first no one was there. She rang the bell, pounded on the door. Finally a tall, neatly dressed woman appeared and slowly unlocked the door. She admitted the caseworker reluctantly into an immaculate living room. The shades were drawn, and the room was dim. Furniture stood at stiff, precise angles as if it had been frozen into position. In one corner expensive toys and dolls were lined up in military array, and their unmarked perfection was mute evidence that no child's hands played with them. Nothing moved in that room. Even when the children returned from school nothing moved. At Mrs. Smith's command they sat rigidly erect on their chairs, and they did not speak.

Mrs. Smith was angry that a complaint had been made, and she blandly denied there was any basis for it. Any marks on the children were clearly the result of accidents incurred when

90

they were playing outside. She was good to the children. When they came home from school she asked them to verify that. With frightened eyes they repeated her statements. She was very good to them, never beat them, and they had hurt themselves while playing.

Now Mrs. Rill talked to relatives, to the children's teachers, to anyone who might help. The relatives said it was true that Mrs. Smith tortured the children. They would like to help but they were afraid; she had threatened to kill them if they interfered. The grandmother wanted to take the children, but she did not dare oppose Mrs. Smith. The teachers could verify that they had seen burns and cuts and welt on the children, but they could not prove how they got them. A neighbor called the caseworker and implored, "Please do something. It's awful. I hear the children screaming and I've seen Mrs. Smith chase them around the yard in the snow in the early morning. They're barefoot, and she makes them run around and around." When Mrs. Rill asked, "Will you testify to that?" the woman refused. She was terrified of Mrs. Smith. She feared the woman would hurt her own children.

Repeatedly Mrs. Rill tried to talk to Mr. Smith. He was never home, responded to no letters or telephone calls. Once she caught him at home by a surprise evening visit, but he told her hastily that everything was fine, Mrs. Smith took good care of the children and he was sorry but he had to leave to attend a meeting. Mrs. Smith was increasingly uneasy. She reiterated how much she loved the children, that she never beat them any more, that there was no problem. When the caseworker asked her about her own life, she had nothing to say beyond the briefest facts. She was born in Detroit, her parents were living, she had a brother. It was as if she had no past, had never been a child. In this Mrs. Smith was like most abusing parents, who do not discuss their childhoods, do not talk about people, give no description of parents, brothers, or sisters.

Mrs. Rill had struck a blank wall. She was convinced Mrs. Smith was abusing and tormenting the children, but she had only denials from Mr. Smith, Mrs. Smith, and the children. She did not attempt to talk with the children even at school. They would not dare to tell her the truth, and questions could only terrify them further when she had no power to protect them. She could take the case to court, but relatives and neighbors refused to testify and their fear was genuine. In court Mrs. Smith could be very convincing, with Mr. Smith to substantiate everything she said. There was a good chance the court would leave the children with her, and this would further damage any influence Mrs. Rill might still have.

She continued to visit Mrs. Smith, to attempt over and over again to elicit some response, some interest even in this cold, grim woman. She had no success. Mrs. Smith grew, if anything, more suspicious, more openly antagonistic. She wanted no agency and no outsider interfering in her home, and she made that fact abundantly clear. She loved the children, she said, and she took good care of them. Mrs. Rill noticed that she never talked about them individually, never called them by name, never mentioned anything they did or did not do. They were simply "the children"—an abstraction that could neither be seen nor heard. She never mentioned her husband, as if he did not exist at all.

About this time one of the boys was rushed to the hospital. He had swallowed some lye. Mrs. Smith said he had taken it by mistake and she had hastened to get medical care for him. There was no proof it was not an accident. The boy lived, and everything was the same as before. Mrs. Rill continued to check into the past history of the family and learned there was an older boy in a correctional institution. He had run away from home repeatedly, had said again and again he did not want to go home. Finally he had been sent to the institution because he did not go to school and had continued to run away.

Mrs. Rill began to visit less often in the home because she felt she was accomplishing little there. Instead she and the school began to watch the children quietly but steadily, waiting to see what would happen. It was dreadful to sit and wait for children to be hurt, but there was no alternative. After two or three months an older brother, who had lived with relatives since the death of his own mother, returned to the Smith family. He was entered in school. Like the other children he was always

in school on time, well dressed, spotlessly clean. Unlike the
other children he had spirit and spontaneity. He was not afraid
to talk to people.

He had been in the school about a month when he asked to
see the school social worker. He told her how dreadful life in
this family really was and that he intended to run away. He was
asking for rescue. The school called Mrs. Rill and together they
planned that rescue. Because this boy was able to trust Mrs.
Rill and the school social worker, he was willing to go to the
police with their help and tell what he had seen. The police
picked up all the children promptly, and they were placed in
a temporary shelter.

Only then did Mr. Smith suddenly appear at the agency to
see Mrs. Rill. He verified everything his older son had said and
explained his own passivity by admitting he was afraid of his
wife. "I was afraid she would kill me," he told Mrs. Rill, "and
I kept hoping someone would do something about the children.
I didn't dare come to see you before." Now, he explained, Mrs.
Smith had left the house, and he didn't know where she was.
He hoped she would never come back.

She didn't appear at the court hearing. The children were
placed in the custody of the grandmother who had wanted for
so long to care for them. Only after months of safety with her
did the children talk to Mrs. Rill about what had happened to
them. They told how their stepmother wakened them in the
morning by beating them with a wire, that she had forced them
to sit for hours without moving, that she had rubbed red pepper
into the genitals of the little girl.

They still woke at night screaming with nightmares that she
had come back. Over and over the little girl asked Mrs. Rill for
assurance that she would be protected from her stepmother.
None of the children asked their father for protection because
they knew he could do nothing. Slowly over the months the
children began to emerge from their living nightmare. The little
girl who had been failing in school began to learn, and to taste
success. The boys who had never played began to play with
other children. They were still fearful, and suspicious of people,
still more likely to accept defeat than to fight for anything they

wanted. Some of the fear and the hopelessness will stay with them for the rest of their lives.

Mrs. Smith disappeared after first destroying all the furniture in the house. She had been defeated by the courage of a boy twelve years old. Only discovery of her behavior and the certain authority of the court had changed her adamant refusal of any outside intervention, and assuredly they had not changed her. Almost nothing had been learned about her past, and as a person she was known only through her vicious behavior. People seemed to be only victims and enemies to her.

Learning more directly from a mother was the experience of another social worker in a mental hygiene clinic. The circumstances were considerably different. Mrs. Jones was in late middle age, and her daughter was grown. The girl was schizophrenic and had been hospitalized three or four times. Mr. Jones was mentally ill and sat passively at home having little contact with anyone. Mrs. Jones had come to the clinic to talk about her daughter whose uncontrolled hatred of her mother had become a cause of alarm. Even as she talked about her daughter's behavior Mrs. Jones was careful to explain that she realized she must have done something wrong to account for her daughter's attitude.

The social worker knew that Mrs. Jones had often said this, but what she had done was never explained. The implication was that Mrs. Jones did not know herself what she had done that was so wrong, but she must have done something to account for the present situation. She explained this repeatedly to the social worker with tears rolling down her cheeks. Yet at the same time her face was curiously expressionless.

Then one day the caseworker said quietly, "You don't have to keep saying this, Mrs. Jones. You know and I know that you don't believe it. And with me you don't need to cry." Mrs. Jones sat suddenly erect, and the tears stopped as if a faucet had been closed. There was sudden interest and surprise in her face. "How long have you known that?" she asked.

She was neither angry or perturbed. The caseworker had not attacked or censured her but simply stated a conclusion matter-of-factly. "With me you can tell the truth. There is no need to

pretend," the caseworker told her. After that she talked often
about what she said and did to her daughter, about the present,
not about the past. Now she tormented with words, not blows.
She liked to tell her daughter how her life was a failure, how
ugly she was, how no one would ever want her. The daughter
retaliated in fury, threatening to kill her mother.

The caseworker listened and then told Mrs. Jones flatly,
"You can't say things like that. You are not to talk to her that
way. Look what happens. You get scared and upset and if
you're not careful, your daughter may attack you." Mrs. Jones
looked at the caseworker consideringly and then she nodded,
"You're right. It's not worth it."

For three years the mother came to the clinic every week.
She enjoyed talking to the caseworker and she listened because
she understood that the tables might well be turned on her if
she didn't control her own impulses to hurt. As she remarked
one day, "I created a monster, didn't I? Now the monster attacks
me." The daughter and the husband had peace because of the
prohibitions the caseworker set.

Mrs. Jones came as close to liking and trusting that caseworker as it was in her nature to do. Yet, she never talked about
her own childhood and only referred to the past in vague and
disconnected remarks. Her silence did not seem so much an
avoidance of painful memories as an indifference to a time that
no longer concerned her. What was past was gone and it was
peopled not even by ghosts. The caseworker said, "She did what
I told her because I always put everything in the light of her
own self-interest. She knew I was right. She liked me in her own
strange way because I knew what she was like and took her on
her own terms. I couldn't change her but I did stop her from
making life quite so miserable for her daughter. It was the only
way I could protect her daughter and ultimately herself. Yet
even after three years I have no real tie with her. If I leave
she will forget me quickly because I will be of no further use
to her. She has been fascinating and amazing to work with
but I have done nothing to change her. The person who could
remember and care about someone else seems to be left out

of her. She's empty and there's a coldness at the core of her personality."

The caseworker who faces abusing parents cannot be afraid of them. They exploit fear and they deride weakness. Neither can the caseworker afford any illusions about them; with intelligence they can be very convincing and remarkably adept at saying what the caseworker wants to hear. Their motives are what they conceive to be their own best interests. Primarily they respect power, and there is substantial indication that they evaluate any caseworker, or anyone else for that matter, in terms of how much power over them that person has. It is a frightening personality type and one not confined to parents. Families like these require the most mature, sophisticated, and experienced caseworkers available, people clear in their purpose and comfortable with authority.

The greatest asset a caseworker can have in dealing with these families is a deep conviction that no one has the right to abuse the helpless. It is because of that conviction, not anger at the parents, that a worker hangs on and fights for the children. It is the kind of stubborn concern that kept one child welfare executive in a police station until midnight. The children's agency had custody of a four year old girl who had been placed in a foster home after the court had removed her from an adoptive home. Her young, unmarried mother had sold her for fifty dollars to a family she met casually. The family had never legally adopted the child but regarded her as their unquestioned possession. They had, after all, bought and paid for her.

They were bitter at the court's decision which had followed their abuse of the child. They were angry at the agency which had placed her and would not tell them where she lived. Finally, the agency consented to let them see her but only at the agency office. They were alone with her for only a few moments, but that was enough. They grabbed the screaming child and ran. The agency called the police and then began checking every possible address where the parents might be.

The executive and the young caseworker started the long,

weary search. Evening came and they went to the police station
with the most likely address to find the parents. It was a while
before the busy precinct could release detectives to accompany
them. They waited. When with the police they found the child
it was midnight. The man was under the influence of drugs. The
woman was openly masturbating the child. The little girl said
nothing until the executive and the caseworker had her safely
tucked between them in a taxi headed for home. Then suddenly
she turned to her caseworker and with anger in her voice asked,
"What took you so long?" It had never occurred to the little
girl that her good friend, the caseworker, would not come. She
was so sure she could afford to be angry that it had taken her
friend so long.

That patient search had done more than preserve a child's
faith in goodness and honesty. When they found her, the
parents were already packed and ready to leave at daylight for
another state. The concern of those two social workers had
saved a child's life. Today that little girl lives in a real adoptive
home with real parents.

The kind of tenacious concern shown in this case has never
been common, and it isn't common today, but it is just about the
most precious thing in the world. Not that those two stopped
to think about their night's work in any such terms. They went
home to bed with the quiet satisfaction of a job well done.

The young children in these families were saved because they
were taken away from those who would hurt them. They may
carry with them the scars of past violence, but they carry also
the hope for a decent and useful life. For Mrs. Jones' daughter
it is too late. All the caseworker was able to do was keep life
more tolerable by continuing to see the mother and to control
her destructiveness. This does not mean that every child growing up with abusive parents will necessarily become schizophrenic. It does mean that no child can live with such destructiveness and not be to a greater or lesser extent destroyed as a
person. Prevention will always be the best cure.

And so it is for neglecting families. The parents are usually
less hostile, less secretive, less belligerent. They may come to
welcome the caseworker as a support, but whether they can use

another person's strength to make a home for their children depends on their own inner strength and hopes. Nor is it easy for a caseworker to offer that strength month after month without growing discouraged.

A young woman sent to investigate a complaint that children were not fed and cared for rapped on the door of the apartment. A woman's voice yelled, "Come in." The caseworker opened the door to find the mother in bed with a man, both of them drunk, and the children, dirty and nearly naked, playing apathetically across the room. The woman, the children's mother, was not perturbed. When the caseworker, who was perturbed, identified herself the woman said cheerfully, "Come right in. I'll get some clothes on. Don't mind him"—pointing to the man in the bed—"he'll sleep." And he did.

The young caseworker tried hard to help this woman become a mother. The trouble was she wasn't very interested in her children. She drank heavily, had a succession of men friends, and fled from responsibility. She liked the caseworker, but that didn't mean she liked responsibility any more than before. As she explained, she went out to do the shopping, had a drink on the way, met people in the bar and forgot about the children. When she took to forgetting them for two or three days, the caseworker went to court. The children were removed.

Neglect cases, however, do not always end that way. The Burns family had been one of those chronic problem families that are always being evicted because they're so dirty and always behind in the rent. The neighbors complained because the children ran wild and their parents never paid any attention to them. The school complained because the children were forever truanting and when they did come, were dirty and half-fed. The parents complained because people wouldn't leave them alone. The children didn't complain. They simply went their own way, stole what they wanted, threw rocks at the neighbors, avoided the school, and in general made themselves into budding delinquents.

Mr. Burns had a steady job and earned enough to support the family, but somehow the money dribbled away with little to show for it. He spent a good bit on himself but as he explained,

"I earned it, I got a right to spend it as I please." Mrs. Burns said bitterly, "How can I cook decent meals when he doesn't give me enough money to buy what we need?" Besides she felt her husband had all the fun while she was cooped up in an overcrowded apartment with no one to talk to and nothing to do but work. When she got too lonely, she went down to the corner bar and drank beer and talked to people. Then there were more complaints.

The Burns family had known several social agencies off and on. Mostly Mr. and Mrs. Burns regarded caseworkers in the same light as neighbors, landlords, and truant officers, people to be avoided when possible and fought off when not. The situation had stayed the same for several years except that the children were getting older and the complaints more frequent. Everyone was convinced that the family was hopeless.

When a new caseworker, a young man, arrived at their door, the parents responded as usual with complaints about each other and their immediate neighborhood. The young man listened and observed. He talked to social workers who had known the family in the past, to teachers, and to the landlord. Then one day he told Mrs. Burns calmly. "You've been blaming the agencies, the school, everyone around you. But you and your husband haven't done much about all this trouble. Your children are getting into trouble with the law, and the community will do something soon if you don't. If you want to keep your children I'll do everything I can do to help you. If you don't care, then I won't go along with any more drifting."

Mrs. Burns was furious. "No one ever talked to me like that," she told the caseworker. "Maybe they should have," was his quiet response. "I will come back tomorrow evening and I want to talk with you and your husband." That interview ended with Mr. Burns saying finally, "All right, what do you want us to do?"

"First, I want you to paint the kitchen. I want Mrs. Burns to plan with me a week's menu's, cook three meals a day, and serve them on a table for the whole family together." The parents agreed, still angry and yet with a certain relief.

In the next few months the neighborhood thought a miracle

had happened. The family cleaned up, took care of the children, sent them to school. Mrs. Burns shopped and cooked and Mr. Burns used his salary for his family. Both parents called the caseworker on every question. Sometimes he told them what to do, and sometimes he said that was a decision they were quite capable of making for themselves. He helped both parents and children join in some community groups. He taught the parents what standards they must maintain and how to do it. The family agreed he was the best caseworker they'd ever met. The neighborhood said the family wasn't so bad after all.

Why did it work? The young caseworker saw correctly that the parents were behaving like children, and he acted like a good parent to them. He was direct and frank but not punitive. He had the patience and good sense to give his attention to the important details and small actions of everyday life. He set the limits of parental behavior but he also opened new doors. The parents liked and trusted him because they knew he was genuinely interested in them. Most important of all they wanted to use help when someone offered the kind of help that they could use. Sometimes, if people can't use the kind of help we offer, we assume they are hopeless. More often we should ask, "are we truly offering what people need?"

Some social workers may question what happens to a concept such as self-determination when a caseworker tells a family what they must do. It is easy to overlook the fact that the family did in effect make a choice and abided by its consequences. That is about all the self-determination that life allows anyone. If the parents had chosen to disregard the caseworker and continue as before, they would have lost their children. It was their good fortune that they had the strength and the help to make a choice that lead toward self-respect.

The children in the Burns family could grow up in their own home. But what about all the children who can't? Even when they're removed for their own protection, don't they still have ties to their own parents? Often we have heard that children would rather be in their own homes no matter how unhappy they may be. This was not a belief shared by many of the children in this study. For example, a little boy with an abusing

father had been placed temporarily. He knew he would have
to return home. When the caseworker came to get him, he
sighed, "So soon? I didn't think I'd have to go back so soon." A
girl of twelve placed in a good foster home was threatened with
return to her abusive mother. The mother had hired a lawyer
and was demanding the return of her daughter. Unless the
child herself had the courage to testify to what had happened
at home, there was a good chance the mother would get her
back. When the caseworker told the girl this, she asked one
question, "Will you guarantee that I'll be taken care of until
I'm grown?" The caseworker could make this guarantee. The
girl testified she never wanted to live with her mother again.
Grownups forget or prefer to ignore how realistic children are;
they know their own weakness and cannot afford to be im-
practical.

The question, do children prefer to live in misery with their
natural parents if they have experienced happiness with foster
parents? is answered clearly in case after case. A severely
neglected little boy was placed in an excellent foster home. His
foster mother came to love him deeply. After several months
his natural mother abruptly appeared for a visit. The child
ran to his foster mother and clung to her in a panic. The natural
mother said angrily, "How can you act like that? I'm your
mother." The child shook his head stubbornly and tightened
his hold on the foster mother, "No, this is my mother."

That little boy raised a serious question. Is his mother the
woman who bore him or the woman who loved and cared for
him? He gave his answer clearly, quickly, decisively. The larger
question remains. We have assumed that the mother who bears
the child also loves and cares for him, and when that is true,
there is no question. With the families in this study that was not
often true. Many of the children were saying in one way or
another, "This is not a home." The real question is—are these
families truly families? What does it take beyond biology to
make a family?

IX: The Family Dilemma

One of the basic question raised by the families in this study is whether human needs take precedence over biological relationships. Biology has always been the basis of the family, but it has never been the only one. As the most vital and enduring of all human institutions, the family has always carried great responsibilities; without it society could not exist, at least in any form recognizable to us. But what happens when the biological ties and the social responsibilities are divorced?

There has been and still is a popular assumption that all parents love their children and that love and care are an inherent part of biological parenthood. In addition, there has been the assumption that children would rather live with their natural parents, no matter how neglectful or abusive, than in the finest substitute home. Neither of these assumptions is true for most of the families in this study.

Another common idea has been that with help from courts and social agencies parents may develop love and concern for their children. Even this was found to be false in this study. Perhaps we do not yet know enough to give the kind of help that would be required. Meanwhile, we need to protect the children who are now growing up in homes of neglect and abuse.

The question is not whether all these children should or should not be removed from their natural parents permanently, but what is the criterion that will be used to determine that decision in any individual case. If it is biology alone, the little boy mentioned in the preceding chapter will be returned to his natural mother regardless of his unwillingness to do so. If it is the social and human needs of the children, he will remain with his foster mother probably permanently. This is a difficult question complicated by strong emotions and powerful assumptions. It is an integral part of the whole question of the "natural rights" of parents which are derived from biological parenthood, not from responsibility and appropriate behavior.

The precise nature of parental rights is anything but clear. Some of the parents in this study said bluntly that their children were their "property" and they could do what they pleased with their own "property." This is clearly to deny human individuality to children and leave them subject to chance for any protection. The English common law said succinctly that "the rights of parents derive directly from the obligations of parents." This adds to rights the requirement of social responsibility. The nature of that responsibility would normally be defined by the culture and the particular society. The parents in this study claimed in effect that their rights over the lives of their children were above and beyond any defined fulfillment of responsibility to them. It is a dangerous philosophy.

To answer this dilemma as some people have done by saying, "Make the parents behave, make them take responsibility," is advice more conspicuous for its simplicity than its practicality. The old axiom that you can drive a horse to water but you can't make him drink has more than casual relevance. How do you make parents carry responsibility short of assigning a permanent custodian to each family? If there are parents incapable of carrying continuing responsibility, as was certainly true of some in this study, what is achieved by a compulsion that cannot compel?

It is easy to blame the parents and forget about the children. It is easy to assume that the modern family is blithely forgetting its great responsibilities. As a matter of fact the family is bombarded with accusations of failure, viewed with alarm as a defaulter of ancient responsibilities, idealized into a semi-mystical nobility, and generally exhorted to improve its ways. It is attacked, defended, lectured, and sold like soap with suitable slogans. There is even a lurking fear that like the stagecoach it may vanish from the national scene, and against that dire possibility we have ready at hand a Madison Avenue facsimile of healthy, smiling parents each leading by the hand a healthy, smiling boy and girl. Neither germs nor problems could penetrate their cellophane-covered perfection.

Yet, the family was around long before the full-page ad and will be around long after the slogans have subsided. The anthropologists can find no time in all of human history when the family did not exist, and Murdock[1] points out, "The nuclear family is a universal human social grouping." He adds that in the nuclear family, that is, father, mother, and children, are "assembled the four functions fundamental to human social life—the sexual, the economic, the reproductive, and the educational. Without provision for the first and third, society would become extinct; for the second, life itself would cease; for the fourth, culture would come to an end." The family—the toughest, the most adaptable, the most vital of all human institutions—has survived the fall of civilizations, the impact of every catastrophe that has befallen mankind, the pressures and demands of every age and society.

In the modern world a change has occurred in the structure and obligations of the family that has brought long-range implications for everyone. Many of the great integrating forces of the past have become casualties of industrial society. The extended family which belonged to an agricultural economy provided more than an answer to the baby-sitter problem. The group of culturally determined relatives that made up the whole family unit provided the past, present, and future for its members. Like the old Chinese family that might have four or even five generations living under one roof, it was the symbol of human continuity, the meaning and the purpose for the individual. What it sacrificed in individual freedom it compensated for in security. The family was large; there were grandparents, aunts, uncles, and cousins ready to carry the responsibility and work for the family as a unit. Its members lived close to each other and shared the benefits and the

[1]Murdock, George M., *Social Structure*, (New York: MacMillan Co., 1949).

burdens. So long as the family unit functioned a mother was not left without support, a father without secure care for his home, the children without relatives to provide them with care and security. The family was social security, protection of children, aid to the aged, the civic club, the family life education, the life insurance. While there is no evidence that universal love among the relatives was any more prevalent then than now, loneliness and the bitterness of solitary anxiety could not have been the gnawing problems they are today.

In that big family group, young parents had not only guides and teachers but they shared responsibility and authority with those members of the family who had been culturally assigned these specific roles. Power and responsibility were specific, not diffused, and because they were determined and enforced by tradition, they were less dependent upon the quality of personal relationships. The young mother might dislike her mother-in-law, but since the duties, powers and obligations of each were carefully defined, there was less chance that their personal feelings would disrupt family unity. Each took it for granted that family unity was more important than personal attitudes and hence adaptation and compromise had the spur of necessity. Nor was that young mother likely to differ in important ways from the ideas and customs of her mother-in-law. Even when they differed in the upbringing of her children, she did not expect to be the sole arbiter or the final authority.

Parents and children lived within a framework built of mutual rights and obligations which covered every aspect of life and which had been charted by the impersonality of culture. While the rules were impersonal, their enforcement was personal. The head of the family group was usually the judge and jury. Other family members were assigned specific and decisive roles according to the particular cultural pattern. Each member of the family knew specifically what his responsibility to the total family was and what in turn he could expect from its other members. He knew who controlled what, who had the final power and the last word. He knew what were the limits, the standards, the guidelines, the areas of leniency, and those of rigid enforcement. Because none of this changed lightly, he tended to take it mostly for granted. Within the charted structure, individual feelings and attitudes might vary and clash, express preferences and antagonisms, but the structure remained constant.

Since privacy was not easily achievable under such circumstances, there was little individual or family behavior that could remain invisible. This meant that family controls were not only powerful but pervasive. The less opportunity for concealment, the more complete was the family control over individual behavior.

This does not mean that child abuse and child neglect are new. While history has left small record of the everyday doings of everyday people, it has left enough for us to know that infanticide can be traced from the ancient world up to the present. Children have been left to starve, sold as slaves. In ancient Rome it was legal for a father to kill his children; it was taken for granted in the old Roman family that the *pater familias* had the power of life and death over his children. They were part of his property. Yet even then there were safeguards built into the society and the religion to restrict the individual parent. The Emperor Hadrian banished a man for killing his son.

In the course of centuries the attitude of the civilized world has changed. Today the parent who kills his child is legally accountable for murder. Society no longer approves parental power without qualification even though in practice there are still parents who behave as if that remained unchanged.

The modern family has become in many ways the opposite of the ancient family. Father, mother, and children constitute an independent unit. Not only do grandparents and relatives have no responsibility and no authority to interfere, it is regarded as morally reprehensible if the young family depends too heavily upon them and is not prepared to "stand on its own feet." Advice may be accepted or rejected, depending more upon the quality of the personal relationships than any mutual rights and obligations; even advice from grandparents is regarded as something of an intrusion upon the individual family unit unless it is specifically solicited. The interfering mother-

in-law is in our culture a subject for wry humor with the implication that the interference is both unwanted and unneeded.

The care and education of the children is the responsibility
of the parents, and relatives have neither the legal nor moral
right to exercise control in this area. Their influence, if any, is
dependent upon the quality of the personal relationships, not
upon any legal rights. Further, relatives may know little about
what happens within the individual family because privacy
is protected. A large area of family behavior is invisible, and
whatever relatives may guess or suspect, there are no constituted channels for verification. Both family knowledge and
family control are pretty much confined to the immediate family
unit.

The modern family has a freedom and an independence impossible under the old extended family structure. It has also the
responsibility commensurate with that freedom. Upon two
people rests the full weight of choices and consequences that
once was shared with a group, and the choices and consequences have grown increasingly complex. Where once the
elders of the family took for granted the right of major decisions, our culture applauds the young parents who make their
own. The wisdom of experience, once so highly cherished, loses
much of its potency in a world so swiftly changing that it may
become today's absurdity and tomorrow's nostalgia. With independence and responsibility has come also a loss of the old
security.

When the welfare of the family rests upon two people, the
loss of one is a major blow. Upon the personal relationship of
two people rests most of the determination of the family's
emotional climate, of the happiness or unhappiness, organization or disorganization of its members. When these two people
tend to be scarcely beyond the stage of adolescence, the demands may be exorbitant. Where once security was woven into
the very fabric of the family, now its chief source is in the
individual strength and maturity of two parents. It is not surprising that the search for security has become one of the major
themes of our time.

The old certainty that so long as the family survived the

individual member of it had a place in the world has yielded more and more to the philosophy that each person makes his own place. It is a philosophy that offers greater opportunities and wider freedoms, but its price is greater anxiety and increasing loss of sure refuge from struggle. With it has come the need for outside help when the inevitable exigencies and weaknesses of any individual life—sickness, old age, sudden catastrophe—come about. Government has accepted the responsibility for financial assistance. Insurance, whether private or state in sponsorship, must now provide protection against the expected and unexpected situations that may deprive individuals of self-sufficiency. Organized groups of all kinds offer those same services to families, to children that were once almost solely the responsibility of the family. Social agencies seek ways of strengthening the internal ties of family life that must now resist the pressures of centripetal forces.

Yet, all of these groups and agencies are impersonal; they are official whether their purpose is profit or service. They have eligibility requirements, administrative procedures, records. Of necessity they are specialized. Each offers one segment of help for one segment of need. Personal concern, personal support, personal guidance are as lacking as personal control. At their best these diversified and specialized groups offer the advantage of knowledge, skill, and resources undreamed of by the old-time family. At their worst they make of human need a card catalogue in a dreary line of metal files. At their best and at their worst they can never give the personal roots that feed inner strength, that assuage life's loneliness. Only personal loyalty and concern can do that. The modern family would probably find intolerable the restraints imposed upon individual volition and freedom of the old, extended family, but the price of freedom and independence comes high.

Yet another great shift has been imposed upon the family by modern society, the shift from tradition to swift adaptability to change. One of the great responsibilities and strengths of the old family was continuity, the bridging of past, present, and future and the guarding of the values, standards, and manners of the culture. When, as in some of the old Chinese households, a child could see three generations before him and as an adult three following him, he could scarcely fail to have a built-in sense of stability and strength of tradition. That this tends to oppose change and to substitute stability for flexibility is self-evident. In modern industrial society it becomes an impossibility. Yet, stability is also a unifying force, and in losing this kind of continuity the family also lost part of its stability. Even the importance of carrying on the family name has tended to diminish until it has become little more than a historical curiosity.

Tradition is the cement of continuity. It prescribes what shall continue, in what form, and by what means. It carries values and goals. It preserves the pride of the past for the education of the future. It gives the significance of time to the actions of the present and the meaning of a defined place in history to the everyday behavior of the individual. Symbols and rituals proudly mark its presence. In the old family tradition was all powerful whether it was the proud and famous tradition of a great family of history or the inconspicuous unity of an inconspicuous family. Continuity and tradition are not lost to the modern family, but they have been pushed into second place by the new gods of change, speed, technological progress, and human adaptation.

The modern age requires qualities of character and temperment in parents that can provide the unifying force upon which the use of the manifold resources must depend. When restraints and supports from the outside are altered and weakened, the internal strength of individual character must substitute for it if some measure of family unity is not to be lost. Personal integrity, loyalty, wisdom, responsibility have become requirements for family strength.

The families in this study lack internal strength and external limits. Like small children with dolls the parents want rights to the children without responsibility for them. Our society has fostered this attitude by continuing to act on assumptions that might have been valid with the extended family but are ill-adapted to the needs and purposes of the modern family. A student from the middle East where the old family structure is still powerful remarked that no agency in her country would see abused children. If parents abused a child, the senior member of the family, in this case the paternal grandfather, would simply remove the child and keep him. What relative has this power in our society? Who substitutes for that relative and by what criterion do we decide that authority is to be implemented?

What do we mean by the rights of parents? What are these rights? We can scarcely mean the right to starve a child or break his arm. Yet one judge returned a four year old boy to the mother who had twisted his arm until it broke because he did not have "sufficient grounds for terminating her parental rights." In practice he was supporting such a supposition. If we say parents have the right to determine the upbringing of their children except when, as with education, society specifically denies volition to them, then we must also stress that parents have obligations to the needs of their children, both in the present and in the future.

Nothing we have done in this whole sad area of child protection has been more disastrous to children than the assumption that rights and responsibilities can be separated. It has encouraged parents already wavering under the burden of their own weakness to greater irresponsibility. It has removed the checks upon the indulgence in sadism of abusing parents. It has caused much of the inconsistency and confusion to be seen in social work practice, in court room decisions, and in the attitude of the general public which has swung from indulgence to angry and impulsive punishment. In breaking the bond between obligations and rights we end by substituting punishment for discipline or by trying to deny the reality of the whole problem.

What consistent responsibilities do we want the family to carry? We want parents to support the children economically. This is an objective none would dispute, but it is no criterion for determining what constitutes a family. One of our great social advances has been the recognition that poverty and human inadequacy are not synonymous, that children should not be removed from their homes for economic reasons alone. We want parents to care for their children physically, to feed them, keep them clean, supervise their activities, protect them from

dangers. This is certainly a basic responsibility of the family.
We want parents to teach their children socially approved
standards of behavior, to provide the guidance and authority
which help children live up to society's expectations. This also
is an ancient responsibility of the family.

Perhaps more than ever before we look to the family to provide the personal concern, the emotional continuity, the qualities of character and conscience which prepare children for
mature adulthood. The protection of the helpless, the security
of the weak belong to the finest ideals for which human beings
have struggled. The passing on of the values of civilization is a
necessity for civilization's survival. There is no substitute for
the family in fulfilling that great responsibility. It has never
been more difficult nor more important.

Many of the families in this study failed to meet these responsibilities in any but the most minimal fashion; many of them
failed even to acknowledge that such responsibilities existed.
The fact of biological parenthood was in itself sufficient and
constituted the seal of possession. For them children were a
commodity, not an obligation. Perhaps nothing so distinguishes
the true family as the conviction that children are people.

We expect biological and emotional parenthood to belong
together and when they do, there is no problem. When, as with
so many neglectful and abusive parents, they do not, the question is which kind of parenthood takes precedence. Many of the
children in these families indicated that parents were those who
cared for and about them. They made their choice abundantly
clear when they asked for "a home." Our society has yet to
give its final answer. Unless it is willing to assume some of the
responsibility, to circumscribe those parental rights which are
blatantly misused, it can do little to protect the children growing up in chaos.

The image of family experienced by these children makes a
mockery of the finest ideals evolved out of human experience
and human aspirations. It is that image and our confusion that
constitute the menace to the true meaning of family. The family
will not be protected or strengthened by a comfortable fantasy
that at heart all parents are pretty much alike and all that is

needed with neglecting and abusive parents is a little guidance
or a stern judicial lecture. The values of the family are too
important, too necessary to be subverted into a slogan, a sta-
tistic, a phantom reality. Its great obligations need more than
ever to be honored and supported. If we deny them whether
out of indifference or confusion, we can have little rationale for
complaint when the children of these families create in their
turn families that are not families.

X: A Preventive Approach

Of all the professions and occupations that share responsibility for helping with some portion of the miseries and tragedies of these parents and children, social work has the most direct and extensive share. It meets families in child welfare agencies, in mental hospitals, children's institutions, on the rolls of public assistance, in hospitals, schools, and courts. Long ago they overflowed the confines of the protective agencies. Dealing endlessly with the results of personal and family disorganization, social work has often failed to recognize the common elements disguised by varying results.

Because over the years social services have grown like a patchwork quilt to answer specific behaviors and problems, they are divided into pieces now not easily integrated. The neglecting mother supervised by the child welfare worker may also be the patient known to the social service department of the mental hospital, the parent known to the court probation officer who works with her child, the client who receives some form of financial assistance from public welfare. She is four different people to four different agencies. Each carries a part of the responsibility, and each tends to perceive her and her children within the confines of that responsibility. The consequence is to obscure both the nature and the extent of the problems.

No one knows how many neglecting and abusing families there are. While this study did not attempt to estimate the number, it turned up one surprising result that may be illuminating. The cases selected at random were expected to provide a small group of families that had needed child welfare services for other reasons than child neglect or abuse. They could for purposes of the study, be compared with cases of neglect or abuse. Of the 38 families so selected, 31 of them or 81 percent differed in no essential from the families chosen because of a complaint of parental neglect or abuse. Although this sample is too small to permit any conclusion, it poses a serious question. Are the majority of families served by child welfare agencies actually protective in nature regardless of the specific mode of their referral? Is the fact of a complaint from the community more of a fortuitous chance, a consequence of locality or of grossness of behavior than a reliable indication of the true extent of neglect and abuse?

If the answers to those questions are affirmative, then child welfare is faced with a major reorientation in its thinking, its approach, its definition of its responsibility. The old questions of voluntary placement of children by parents, of family rehabilitation, of temporary placement of children must all be reconsidered. Protective services must move from a specialized peripheral place to the central core of child welfare responsibility. The importance of learning the answers to these questions is self-evident.

Equally important is the need to determine the extent of protective cases. Nor does the question of the size of this problem rest solely with child welfare. It cannot even be estimated reliably until it is traced through courts, mental hospitals, correctional institutions, children's hospitals. In short, social work must handle the barriers of its divided and specialized responsibilities if it is to learn the actual impact of the protective problem and the extent of its ramifications. From all the present evidence it is much greater in size than we had imagined, much more deadly in its consequences than we had conceived.

The next question is, logically, what is social work to do about it? Since social workers deal primarily with individual families, with the persons directly concerned rather than with the underlying social causes or the broad sweep of sociological setting, the answer must derive from the specifics of individual work with individual families. It was not the purpose of this

study to evaluate the effectiveness of the methods now used
in working with neglecting and abusing families, but the records were abundantly clear that our present methods are not
achieving solutions. Caseworkers struggle against overwhelming personal and social pathology. Without adequate resources,
community understanding, or even professional recognition
from their own field of the severity of the problem, they meet
the ever-recurrent crises with such improvised means as are
available to them. All too often they watch their best efforts
dissolve into chaos.

In many public agencies caseworkers must carry workloads
far in excess of the capabilities of any person however knowl-
edgable and experienced. Working with gross disorganization
they are by the sheer weight of the demands upon them
compelled into a weary and futile treadmill that is in turn
disorganizing. Many of these caseworkers are young, from
middle-class backgrounds, nurtured in the easy optimism of
success. They are plunged into a human jungle where the sordid
is commonplace and defeat has the stamp of finality. Into
houses where the threat of violence hovers like Poe's Raven
they bring the uncertainties of their own anxiety, their own
confusion of what is expected of them, their own self-doubts
and tenuous preconceptions. It is not surprising that few of the
families in this study had the same caseworkers for so much as
a year.

Even when agency circumstances were more favorable there
was a continual changing of workers. This fact in itself is disastrous to effective help for disorganized families. To the confusion of their lack of continuity the agency introduces yet
another discontinuity. The results were apparent in many of
the recorded cases which showed growing indifference of parents and children to agency intervention, and unchecked deterioration. While there are a number of reasons for this staff
transiency—some of them not easily alterable—a good number
of the caseworkers said that the apparent futility of their efforts
was one of the chief causes of change for them. Working with
families as pathological as these is neither easy nor pleasant,

and when from all appearances it is also futile, there can be little incentive to continue.

That futility has proceeded from three sources. There have been no clear diagnostic classifications by means of which a family's potential for change might be predicted with any accuracy. Secondly, the assumptions on which most casework methodology is based have not been examined for their relevance to the specific needs and problems of this group. Third, the general tendency in casework has been to regard treatment as primarily psychological in nature; to see work with a heavily environmental emphasis as more reminiscent of casework's past than representative of its present. The individual caseworker, therefore, too often faces the problems of neglecting or abusing families with no clear definition of a possible goal, no specific guidelines as to what means he should use, and little professional conviction that he can achieve the kind of results he feels should ensue.

The question of predictability is yet to be solved and in any truly scientific sense will be enormously difficult to answer. Yet the alternative, to begin every case as if it were so different that experience has no relevance, is to concede defeat. For a long time humanity has been making use of the patterns of experience and while they are sometimes fallacious and usually faulty, they have also given great service. Casework uses them constantly, sometimes to its sorrow but often greatly to the benefit of those it seeks to serve. The diagnostic classifications in this study have been based upon patterns of visible behavior, and while they cannot be used in themselves as predictive indicators of results, they may in combination with the resources of experience cast some light upon probable consequences and hence upon possible goals.

None of the cases in the severe abuse group in this sample showed any visible change toward a more constructive way of life so long as the family members remained together. The only qualification of this devastating conclusion was in the few situations where a strong caseworker placed a prohibition on parental abuse to which the parents conformed at least out-

wardly and temporarily. It was not possible from this study to
know how effective that prohibition was in behavior not visible to the outside nor how permanent its effects. Since there
was no discernible change in parental attitude, it seems likely
that the effectiveness of the prohibition is tied to the continuing
activity of the caseworker. In all the other cases progress resulting in greater protection for the children followed only when
the abusing parent was out of the home or the children had
been placed away from the parents.

Rarely in these families did the abusing parent leave voluntarily, and most often the passive partner clung frantically to
the existing situation regardless of its persistent misery. Only
when the children were older—and usually too late for them—
or when some external situation intervened, such as a parent
going to prison, was there a break in this chain of pathology.
When the children were placed out of the home, it was usually
by court action. In a number of cases the court made only temporary placements and returned the children when the parents
requested it; in none of these cases was there any change in
parental behavior. The children were, if anything, worse off,
and their behavior, in a number of cases, deteriorated rapidly.
The hope that parents like these will "come to their senses" if
the children are removed for a few months can spring only
from an ignorance of the nature of their pathology.

If the behavior of the parents in this sample is true generally
for severely abusing parents, then the goal of casework must be
permanent removal of the children from the home. This may
seem a drastic and shocking objective, but to torture and deliberately inflict misery on helpless children is also drastic and
shocking. The questions may well be raised, should not ameli-
orative measures always be attempted first? Are there not
methods yet untried to alter or at least mitigate this kind of
parental behavior? To the first question one can only say that
always the facts must be known, studied, and documented, but
beyond that amelioration can be attempted only for a limited
time when the price of failure may be the suffering or death of
a child. As for the second question, there can be no doubt that
to seek new and effective means of mitigating parental be-

havior is of primary importance. The amount of human suffering that would be prevented is tremendous. What has to be faced at the present is the fact that we are not accomplishing enough with existing methods.

If they are removed from their homes, child welfare must answer the question of where children are to be placed. To this question also there is no easy answer. Placement resources diminish rather than increase, and they become steadily more costly. Yet, to say that resources are inadequate to meet the need does not negate the need nor the responsibility to seek such resources. One agency that has been removing children from abusive homes wherever possible has learned that in a number of cases responsible relatives have been willing to take the children when they were assured that the parents could not intervene and take the children back. It is a partial answer only, but every possibility is life and hope for another child.

Some of the children could be placed for adoption. In one of the cases in this study a little boy had been terribly abused by his severely pathological mother. He had been placed in a foster home and returned to his mother at her request. When the caseworker found him the second time he was in bed, too weak from starvation to stand. She bent over him and whispered, "Do you want me to take you out of here?" Weakly the child whispered, "Yes." She placed him in a carefully chosen foster home, and with the foster parents she fought through with him the period of turmoil and confusion that followed. She also secured a legal surrender of custody from his mother. When he was eight she found an adoptive home. By carefully planned accident she and the little boy met the adoptive parents as allegedly casual friends during a visit to the zoo. When they parted, the boy asked anxiously, "Do they want me?" The worker asked gently, "Do you want them?" Suddenly the child's face relaxed in a grin. "If they want me, they can have me." They wanted him, and one little boy found a real home and a real family.

With parents in the severe neglect group the feasible goals consistent with protection of the children may or may not mean their permanent placement. Many of the parents studied in this group were alcoholics. Psychotic breakdowns were not uncommon. Many of the parents said openly they wanted to be free of the responsibility of their children. Failure to feed children is serious, destructive behavior, and to modify pathology of such severity is certainly no simple task. The vital question is, Is it possible? In the cases in this study no modification appeared so long as the children were young and remained in the home. In some of the families as the children grew older the parents showed more stability. The lessening of parental responsibility may well be the crucial factor here.

Interestingly, in some of the cases where children were placed out of the home the parents did modify their behavior. They were more responsible in their commitments to the children and the agency, but these commitments were limited ones. They fell far short of assumption of responsibility for the care of the children. This change in behavior occurred when one other circumstance was present. Either the children's foster parents or the caseworker responded to the childlike needs of the parents. The parents were more childish than their own children in their dependence, their wish for attention, their narcissism. Relieved of too heavy responsibility, accepted as they were, given some interest and concern, they tried like good children to please those who had helped them, to use the strength they did possess to assist rather than thwart help for their children.

This may seem a limited goal, one that neither prevents permanent placement of the children nor promises any decisive change in the parents. It is none-the-less a goal worth working for when it means a better life for the children and a greater opportunity in turn for their children. In one family a strong caseworker fought hard to bring some order into a chaotic situation where six children existed as best they could with an alcoholic mother and a father who deserted them intermittently. When the father left the home completely, the mother showed a little improvement. When the caseworker took the mother alone on a short picnic, the mother said happily it was the first time she had ever had such a treat. On the way home she suddenly remarked, "I wish you'd take the other children on a picnic too." The "other children" were the six she had borne.

This caseworker took the mother to medical clinic since she, like her children, was half-starved. An interesting development followed. Although there was adequate income for food, the mother seemed unable to do the things that would translate the money into provisions for herself and her children. She refused to take the vitamins given her "for fear I'll get hungry." She finally confessed to the caseworker that she had an aversion to food, to feeding anyone including herself. This mother only ate with relish when she was fed. Not long afterward she had a psychotic breakdown. Despite delusions she called the caseworker first, asked her to come and take her to the hospital and to provide for the children. Now the children are living with relatives, and with the caseworker's help they are finding a security they did not know existed. The older child said recently, "Why couldn't this have happened sooner? They [meaning his younger brothers and sisters] have so much more than I did." The mother, soon to leave the hospital, asked the caseworker hopefully, "Could you find a home for me?" She had refused before to let the relatives take her children. Now she leaves their welfare to the decision of the caseworker and seeks care for herself.

This caseworker has no sense of futility with this family. On the contrary, she knows it represents success. Her goal was limited to the possible, and the results may be far-reaching. The children have a home for the first time in their lives. Their mother has a hope, however, fragile. The work with the family may have pointed the way to important new knowledge that can be studied in other neglecting families. No amount of financial help can answer a problem that finds its expression in an aversion to feeding. But how many of these families in the severe neglect group can be helped to create a home with even the most minimal stability is a question which has yet to be answered.

It is likely that more hopeful are families in the moderate neglect and moderate abuse groups. They show more strength, their pathology is less extreme. There are indications in the records that these parents can be helped to carry necessary responsibility on a continuing basis, that children can be given a better chance within their natural home. In one family, even without continuing casework help, a mother of the moderate neglect type found her way to a more stable pattern of life because she made a good marriage and found some security. For her younger children at least she was able to give structure and direction. She would have made that progress at less cost to herself and her children if she had had help when she needed it most.

What is necessary with all these families if casework is to fulfill its own potentiality for service is a clear purpose that takes priority over all other considerations: protection of the children. It may be too late for many of the parents to achieve maturity, but it is not too late for the children; what cannot be corrected in this generation may be prevented in the next. To spend precious time and energy upon what cannot be done may be to rob the future of what could have been done. We must acknowledge what we do not know as well as what we do know, we must do what lies within our power without denying its limitations but also without denigrating its worth. To permit the sadistic indulgence of pathological parents where it lies in our power to check it is to sacrifice the children to no purpose and to give tacit acquiescence to a crime. To insist that infantile parents carry the responsibility of mature adults is to crush both them and their children and to compound, not solve the problem.

Protection of the children in these families can only be properly implemented by acceptance of the facts. Whether casework planning should be directed toward permanent removal of a child from the family or toward greater integration of the family members is not a decision that should rest with personal biases, preconceived assumptions, or idealized aims, however lofty, that have small chance of realization. The decision in every case rests on the answers to two questions. What constitutes minimally adequate care for children, the level below which the home is so destructive that children can only be seriously and permanently damaged in character, personality, and behavior? Secondly, in what homes can change toward greater family integration take place within the time limits set by the inexorable rate of children's physical and psychological growth?

While neither of these questions can be answered at this point with complete accuracy and reliability, we do know some part of the answers. Child care in severely abusing and severely neglecting homes is far below any civilized level of adequacy. While a standard of adequacy certainly requires more comprehensive and detailed study than this, nevertheless minimum standards would go a long way in helping these children. Further we know that to help the pathological parents in these two groups to the point where they can carry continuing responsibility and make realistic decisions with regard for the welfare of those dependent upon them is not a promising goal within any feasible time limits. This is asking for far more than the surrender of certain kinds of undesirable behavior; it is asking for some strength and maturity expressed in positive and continuing action. Experience has given us small reason up to now to expect such a result from any of the known methods of treatment.

Therefore, our goals for these families must have one objective: protection of their children. The form and requirement of that protection is dependent upon accurate diagnosis and the clearest guide to that is still past and present behavior. Our evaluation of potential for future improvement in behavior must use the light of much collective experience, while carefully considering the degree of danger to the children. This imposes heavy responsibilities upon caseworkers and the burden of decisions which may not be reversible. Only knowledge and conscience can help them.

Methods of working with families like these are dependent, as are all methods, upon purpose and diagnosis. What is the problem? What do we want to do? Given the realities of both, what can we do? Casework methods in general are based upon certain concepts and assumptions. From the records used in this study it seems clear that some of the assumptions are in practice creating confusion and failing to achieve their purpose.

Whether the confusion is primarily the result of misinterpretation of assumptions is not always clear.

In general, casework has tended to focus on the purpose of helping people to effect internal psychological change which in turn would modify behavior and result in personal environmental change. In other words, psychological change was assumed to be antecedent to situational change. There can be no argument with this as a desirable goal. Change within the person is the only kind of change that can offer ultimate solution. The question is, Is it a feasible goal with many if not most of the neglecting and abusing families? While casework practice has never concentrated on psychological to the exclusion of environmental change, it has emphasized that aspect to the point where many workers seem to take it for granted that if this approach fails, there is little hopeful alternative.

Obviously any kind of internal change toward greater maturity depends upon personal motivation. The person must want or come to want a change in his own life situation for which he is willing to pay the price of personal responsibility and personal effort. With most of the parents in this study this motivation was lacking. Their recurrent theme was a longing for change in the other person. One of their central problems was failure to recognize the reality of responsibility and to accept its demands. They sought the freedom of maturity without its accompanying obligations.

Further, any degree of personality modifications presupposes some internal structure capable of modification. It requires the personality strength to absorb the stresses and strains of change and to achieve a new balance, a new integration both within the person and between him and his environment. In most of the parents in this study such inner structure was so fragile and so incomplete that it could not absorb modification. In other words, the psychological approach attempts truly to rehabilitate, "to restore to a former state of balance," according to the dictionary. It is precisely the lack of "a former state of balance," even in an incipient phase, that constitutes the greatest obstacle to rehabilitating these families.

Both experience and logic point to the need for a change in

the focus of approach and in the modification of its purpose. If the assumption of change is reversed to the expectation that external change will precede internal change, at least new alternatives are made possible. Such an approach begins with the facts of external environment, with the attempt to build external structure for the family. Difficult as this is, it lies to a greater degree within the power and resources of casework and is more compatible with the psychological realities of the parents themselves.

External structure is normally made up of the overt behavior expected of any person by the culture of his particular group or society. Rights and obligations are defined, and expectations are enforced formally and informally by the agents of the culture. These expectations correspond to the sociologist's concept of role. With the parents in this study roles were neither defined nor accepted, and parental rights were largely divorced from parental obligations. The lack of standards of behavior and the lack of continuity—insurance of confusion and family distintegration—were common factors in all the groups.

The casework approach would need to begin with the simplest necessities of family life. Probably everyday routine is the most sensible of these. Routine is the structuring of the necessary activities of daily life so that we know what to expect and when to expect it; it gives the security of the familiar and the strength of continuity. It is in itself a form of organization and hence doubly important for disorganized families. For those in this study its most important aspect may be meals which are cooked, put on the table and eaten at certain specified times by the whole family. This is particularly relevant for severe neglect families where there may never be a meal put on the table. One seventeen year old girl, placed at her own request in a foster home, said she had never until then sat down at a table and eaten an entire meal. What the family eats, what it buys at the store, how food is prepared are all important concerns for the caseworker if the children are to be fed. Many of the mothers lack the most elemental knowledge of nutrition as well as the will to act. One mother insisted she fed her children well. She bought potato chips and Coca-Cola regularly.

Cleanliness is another everyday necessity for health as well as organization of family life. Again the specific details of when, how, and what to clean must be the concern of the caseworker if a routine is to be established. A generalized admonition to clean up the house is likely to be futile. Clothing needs washing and care, and the children need to be clothed in the house as well as out, particularly in cold weather in drafty houses and apartments. Many small youngsters are left to run about with little clothing even when it is available and they are suffering from cold.

Obviously these specifics apply only to families where physical neglect is present, but they illustrate the kind of precise, detailed attention that is required in any area of living where disorganization exists, whether it is in the use of money, the behavior of children, the nature of parental recreation, or the scheduling of family activities. They all require the judgment, responsibility, and continuing concern of the caseworker. They constitute the building blocks from which the framework of everyday organized living is built. In normal people they are the outward reflection of inner organization. With these families they must be superimposed from the outside. They are in effect built around the weakness of the parents.

The logical question, of course, is how can they be imposed unless or until the parents want such help or can respond to such an imposed structure. There is one need in many of these parents that makes such a motivation possible: the need and longing to be dependent upon someone who is able to see them as they are and still be concerned for them. Their need for dependence is so great that it can become a focal point for whatever strengths they do have. Like children they respond to strength which substitutes the reality judgment of maturity for the distorted perspectives of their immaturity, that shares the too heavy responsibilities, that makes the everyday rules within which they can find some direction.

As the mother who wanted the "other children" to enjoy a picnic demonstrated, a large ratio of these parents are children psychologically. Their dependence, their inability to carry continuing responsibility, their distorted judgment, their impulsive behavior, their lack of consistent inner controls, their extensive narcissism, are all characteristic of small children. For small children these are normal characteristics but for adults they are not. Casework has sometimes forgotten its own basic rule, "accept people as they are," and in its wish to change them into what they ought to be has minimized the reality of that childishness. The parents have interpreted this often as further rejection, and have responded with indifference or active hostility.

The caseworker who insists upon treating a neglecting parent as an adult, finds that he has no relationship with that parent. No amount of financial assistance or continuing contacts is likely to alter the hostility and indifference that grows up between them. In the records of this study there were many such situations where with the best will in the world a caseworker saw his efforts evaporating into nothing and the family continuing to deteriorate. He wanted the parents to take responsibility, to fulfill their obligations to their children. They wanted the caseworker to be concerned about them, to make the decisions and carry the responsibility for them. As one mother expressed it, "You're always talking about the children, what they ought to have. I want you to talk about me, what I need." One can certainly say with justification that that is not the way it ought to be, but that is the way it is.

The neglecting parents who were able to make a dependent relationship to a caseworker were those who also tried to live up to what the caseworker wanted them to do. They took better care of their children because the caseworker took better care of them. Their dependence, frequently excessive at first, gradually became at least somewhat more controlled as they learned what they could do for themselves. Like children they wanted to please the person who was good to them and therefore they were willing to follow the standards of behavior set up by the caseworker. Contrary to the expectations of many caseworkers they wanted to be told what to do so long as they were convinced the caseworker was concerned for them, and they resented the one who told them, "Of course it is your decision." They wanted borrowed strength, not freedom of choice—a freedom they lacked the strength to use. The only relationships between parents and caseworkers in the records of this study were of this kind.

Another element in these relationships was the professional authority of the caseworker. Clearly if one accepts dependence, then authority is inherent in the situation. In recent years casework has tended to move away from the use of authority, probably in reaction to the days when it was often both punitive and prejudiced in nature. In so doing it lost sight of the distinction between personal and professional authority. Personal authority may be irresponsible, may be a reflection of personal biases, may even with good intent intrude upon that which is none of its business. Professional authority, while subject to all the human weaknesses of those who implement it, is confined by the structure of its purpose, disciplined by its responsibility and accountability, directed by professional knowledge. In casework it is authority used to protect those who are unable to protect themselves. To relinquish it can be only to cripple that power to protect.

Authority has too often been confused with punishment. The expectation of some caseworkers that parents could only resent their authority and thus oppose their efforts springs very probably from this confusion. Actually no one could survive in any society without authority. The traffic light on the corner is authority, and traffic would be an impossible chaos without it. The crucial point is always the purpose of the authority, and that purpose determines the means by which it is implemented. With protective families its purpose is protection of the children, and this by no means implies or necessitates punishment of the parents. It does mean restricting the destructive activities of the parents and when this is impossible, seeking the authority of the court in removing children from the reach of those activities. It is in fact a professional obligation, one not easy to fulfill but of overwhelming importance to many children.

With neglecting parents the use of protective authority is usually a relief. It lifts the weight of responsibility from them, protects them against their own confusion as well as from

the consequences that would ensue from the unchecked expression of their destructive impulses. It is often their first
encounter with consistent strength. Punishment they have been
familiar with a long time, but strength has too often been unknown. Even when they grow angry at the limits imposed by
authority, they show obliquely, like children, that they are glad
it is there. One father became very angry at a caseworker who
set some realistic limits to his behavior and held to them. He
shouted at the caseworker, but he conformed to the limits. A
supervisor who did not understand became alarmed and
changed the family to another caseworker. The father called
the supervisor and asked indignantly, "Can't I get mad and yell
at my worker without losing her? She's the best caseworker we
ever had and we want to keep her."

With the parents in the severe abuse group the reaction to
casework help, including the use of authority, was different.
There was no evidence in the records that the parents made any
relationship with any of the caseworkers. Suspicious, secretive,
hostile, they did not discuss anything personal if they could
avoid it. Wherever it was possible, they manipulated the caseworker and the agency to achieve their own ends. While they
failed to carry responsibility in one or more areas, overt physical neglect of the children was not necessarily one of those
areas. They did not demonstrate dependence upon the caseworker. They tended, therefore, to lack the motivation that
was present with some of the neglecting parents to change their
behavior and at the same time the areas where structure was
lacking were far less accessible to outside observation and
intervention.

It is much easier to develop a daily routine of living with
parents who respond as children than to stop physical abuse of
children by parents who seem to measure all intervention by
the extent of the power it represents. By and large abusing parents were respectful to those they feared, manipulative with
those they could use, and indifferent to everyone else. None of
these reactions are conducive to the development of a relationship and none are promising of much change in parental
behavior. The most effective approach observable in this study

was a quiet, consistent, and persistent use of authority which prohibited the child abuse. It was the strength of the caseworker, not the strength of a relationship which determined how effective that prohibition was. Even under the most favorable situation it was difficult to know whether such a prohibition continued when the family doors were locked and there was no one to observe.

Even if it were reasonably successful, it obviously leaves a great deal to be desired as a solution to the problems of the children. A menace held in check is still a menace, and for young children particularly the terror may be little abated when the controls against parental cruelty are only sporadically visible. If professional authority is used to remove the children, there is a much greater chance of achieving genuine and lasting protection for them.

Many caseworkers may question how realistic their authority can be when it has no legal status and no means of enforcement. Surprisingly, in cases where the caseworker was not afraid and where his authority rested upon the strength of conviction, it was realistic and powerful. The abusing parent became afraid, not of the caseworker as a person but of the caseworker as a symbol. Strength that was used to protect, not to punish; prohibitions that were defined by a standard of morality not by personal whim or bias; conviction that was rooted in concern for the helpless, not in personal gain, realism that sought a solution without need for revenge were qualities that abusing parents did not understand. They represented something unknown and for that reason, frightening.

While examples of this approach were too few to permit any valid conclusions, those that were reported indicated some interesting possibilities. The abusing parent who learned that the caseworker was not afraid and could be neither manipulated nor pushed out of the situation tended to conform at least temporarily to the limits set. In one such case even the caseworker's suggestion that an abusing father take his wife out to a movie now and then was promptly complied with by him as if it had constituted an order. His motivation was fear, not a wish to please, as his wife subsequently observed to the worker.

It was not the initial intervention that precipitated change but the continued intervention that could be neither ignored nor manipulated nor eradicated. Pathology, like health, can find a balance. The caseworker's continued intervention upset the family balance of power. In those few cases where it was possible to know the consequent development, the abusing parent became indifferent to his family in what appeared to be an approximate ratio to his loss of power. In other words when he could not control, he was no longer interested in his children. Much experimentation and concentrated work will have to be done before the possibilities of these observations can be explored and their efficacy proved or disproved. The important fact is that possibilities do exist.

They do not point in the direction of family stability and integration. They seem more likely to result either in the breakup of the marriage, the placement of the children, or both. They do not preclude the necessity of court action and legal authority. They may not in consequence sound like very desirable possibilities. Social workers, like the general public, need to face the reality that maintenance of families like these must in most cases be at the expense of the children, and the goal of preserving the marriage will not result in the popular image of a happy, unified family group.

With parents of the moderate neglect and moderate abuse groups, however, an approach that begins with the building of external life structure may well have a success that can both stabilize the family and promote greater maturity and integration. The acceptance of parental dependence, the sharing of parental decisions and responsibility, the consistency of professional and protective authority may well implement the steps by which these families can conform to standards of behavior acceptable to our society.

The purpose of casework is to bridge the dreadful personal and social isolation. Moderately abusive and neglectful parents cannot by themselves build such a bridge, but since they have some inner strength, there is the possibility of creating it if they get the right kind of help at the right time. The caseworker who helps such a family achieve one success helps that family set in motion the impetus that may lead to many others. This does not mean that with the first step the rest will follow automatically, and the agency which closes the record with a notation of success may be sorely disappointed. No one knows to what extent standards and controls are incorporated within the personality structure of the parent thereby becoming self-perpetuated and self-enforced. Certainly the process of achieving such incorporation would not be quick or easy with adults.

Yet regardless of the time it would require or even whether in many cases it can ever be totally achieved the most important fact is that with persistent help many of these families may bring up their children with standards of behavior and values that the children can make a part of their life patterns. Sharing parental responsibility until the children are grown is a small price to pay for salvaging the lives of children who can be contributors to society, and for breaking the chain of isolation, failure, and dependence.

For casework as a whole the problems and life patterns of these families require that existent assumptions, methods, and goals be studied in the light of their applicability and adaptability. The work with disorganized families in St. Paul, the emphasis on "aggressive casework," the growing stress on educational processes, the renewed awareness of the importance of social environment as a focus of treatment are all evidence that social agencies are already aware of the problem and are reanalyzing premises and methods. As David Hunter of the Ford Foundation has pointed out, "Social agencies have a real problem of holding themselves accountable before the public for what they claim to do."

To meet the problems of these families, the concept of self-determination must be defined and clarified in order to free workers from implied contradictions with the use of professional authority. Casework must broaden its concept of motivation to include any human need that can, with direction, propel people toward a more constructive way of life even when such motivation, as with chronic dependence, is not one approved by our culture. It must differentiate clearly between ideal goals and possible goals and base its actions and plans

upon the possible even as it pursues the ideal. To help a family
that inflicts physical torture upon its children to become a
mature, loving family group is "a consummation devoutly to be
wish'd," but at this point in time it is not a very likely one. Casework must fight with single-minded tenacity against the tempta-
tion to confuse "what is" with "what ought to be" and "how it
came to be." The miserable childhoods and bitter life experiences of most of these parents may go far to explain how they
became the kind of people they are, but that does not alter
what they have become nor negate the damage they inflict upon
their children. Knowing their history helps us to understand
them, but it does not lift our obligation to protect their children.

  Most of all casework must be willing to try out new ways
without sacrificing all that is valid and useful in the old. The
contributions of role theory do not have to imply any contradiction with the insights of psychoanalysis. Focus upon
external structure does not mean that casework has nothing to
offer to those with the strength for internal change. The fact
that one family needs someone to make decisions for them does
not mean that every family does. The great need is for precise,
validated diagnostic patterns and the imagination, flexibility,
and creativity to adapt the goals and methods of treatment
to the specific limits and requirements indicated by the diagnosis.

  Out of specialization and its barriers to perspective, casework
needs to strive for the synthesis of knowledge that would bring
much-needed new information on the extent and nature of
parental neglect and abuse. Such a synthesis would offer new
ways of seeking answers. Group work and casework together,
for example, have already pointed a new direction for helping
these families to learn how to act and interact in a group, with
the hope that some of them may be able to take the independent
step into a community group. Observations of the protective
agency may add to the effectiveness of the social service department of the mental hospital and in turn that department may
contribute to and learn from the public welfare division.

  In facing honestly the challenge of these families, casework
has a brutal job and a tremendous opportunity. It can give a

service to the society that may reflect itself for generations to come. The knowledge it gains may throw light ultimately upon that most serious of all human problems, destructiveness. Its workers will require courage, toughness, the human concern that surmounts the sentimental images of need, and perhaps most important of all, the maturity to take responsibility and live with it comfortably.

XI: The Public Must Help

In the stacatto tempo of everyday urban living most people are aware largely of the bits and pieces of life that swirl around them with accustomed familiarity. The places where they work, shop, the neighborhoods where they live, the restaurants, parks, places of pleasure and recreation set the limits of everyday environment. Their attention is naturally absorbed by their own concerns and those of the people they know. The families described in this book may seem almost as remote from their own lives and concerns as famine in the Far East.

Yet these families walk our streets; their children go to our schools; their problems throng into our hospitals, courts, and social agencies. They are a part of our society, but too often they are as isolated from its main stream as if they lived on a desert island. Those who live in the slums of our large cities are hedged between the glittering prosperity of the commercial center and the tree-shaded comfort of the suburbs. They have no normal contact with either. They may look but not touch. Even when they are not slum-dwellers they remain apart, isolated by their problems and failures. In a group-focused society they do not often join groups. In an achievement-proud culture they have a long record of failure.

This isolation is dangerous. It is dangerous for society and for both the parents and children of these families. With their tendency to have many children, their number increases rapidly. A growing group of families lives in the midst of our society, divorced from the standards of behavior, values, and goals of our culture. Many of them are without hope for any change

133

and without incentive to try either for themselves or their children. The very fact that they can see around them a way of life so different may contribute to their problems. Too often they have nothing to lose, and people with nothing to lose do not often make a contribution to stability. Economically they add to the cost the independent must pay for the dependent. As human beings their misery is a question mark to the assumption of social progress. For the future their homes are a breeding ground of mental illness, delinquency, chronic dependence, unemployability.

If the results of this study are valid for neglecting and abusing families as a whole—and this is a good probability—then our major efforts must be directed toward prevention. Whatever we may be able to achieve with the parents—hopefully we will learn to do much more—the greatest possibilities of change will come with the children. They are still looking for something better, still accessible in most cases to healthy influences, still capable of becoming stronger parents than those they knew. Prevention is easy to talk about but enormously difficult to accomplish. No one would argue its advantages, but many people may be reluctant to pay its cost. Cost, however, accompanies advantages.

The first step in prevention is to know much more about these families than we now know. Much money and energy can be wasted if we attempt to deal in piecemeal fashion with human problems in a vacuum. Problems are attached to people, and the people have patterns of behavior that can be grouped and classified by certain common elements. No two persons will be exactly alike but neither will they be totally unlike. When we perceive the mental illness of some of the parents as one problem, their treatment of their children as another totally separate problem, their unemployability as still another, it is tantamount to not seeing the forest for the trees. When we begin with the family and its individual members who may have one or all of these problems, we begin with a possible focus for prevention.

One of the facts that emerges clearly from this study is that neglecting and abusing parents are two different groups, different in behavior and different in their potentials for the future. Although they have been grouped together legally and generally regarded as belonging together, in fact, they are different kinds of people and require different approaches. Abusing parents may or may not neglect their children physically, depending probably upon their social and economic class, but neglecting parents do not abuse their children. Both groups do share one behavior of considerable importance in any plan of prevention: they do not ask for help with their family problems. They have to be discovered by someone or some agency in the community, and intervention in their affairs is the result of concern from the outside, not of parental volition. By and large the parents seek outside help only for economic need or in some drastic family crisis. It is not clear that they even perceive the family behavior as a problem. For many of them the problem is community pressure and interference.

Thus, preventive planning must begin with identification of these families by schools, hospitals, doctors, courts, and social agencies. The earlier that identification is made, the better the chances of preventive efforts. This necessitates more widespread knowledge about these families and more widespread assumption of responsibility by persons and agencies coming in contact with them. This does not necessarily mean intervening in the family situation directly, but it does mean taking responsibility for reporting the situation to the duly constituted authorities. Inertia that finds its expression in the principle "Never get involved" permits human tragedies to develop and perpetuate themselves. To mind one's own business can be a very sensible practice, but it leaves unanswered the question, When parents fail to protect their own children, whose business is it?

One concerned and conscientious woman listened to the screams of a baby being brutally beaten by his father until she could no longer endure it. Then she knocked on the apartment door and told the father she would call the police if he beat the child again. The father was furious and told her to mind her own business. The other neighbors told her the same thing. Why, they asked, did she have to get involved? She would have been better advised to call the proper agency and report it, but she didn't know what the proper agency was nor what procedure she could follow. No one tried to help her find out. They did not want to be involved, and they did not want her involving them. If the baby died as a result of the beatings, the death would probably be attributed to accident. The question remains, Who is responsible? The answer can only be everyone who knew about it and failed to take any action; we are, after all, responsible for what we don't do quite as much as for what we do. Only through individual responsibility can the children of neglect and abuse be found and be protected. This responsibility falls most heavily upon those professional groups most apt to come in contact with these children.

Doctors, for instance, see many cases of abuse and are probably the only ones who can regularly identify abuse of young children, particularly when the parents are middle-class. Leading physicians are tremendously concerned about the number of murders and serious injuries of infants and young children by parents. They know that many of these deaths and injuries are labeled *accident* and filed away. An outstanding group of doctors have devised means through the use of X rays by which inflicted injuries may be clearly distinguished from true accidents. In so doing they have cleared a major legal obstacle to identification of these families and to means of taking protective action. Medical associations, the United States Children's Bureau, and other concerned groups are promoting legislation that would require mandatory reporting by doctors of all such deaths and injuries to the proper authorities. Several states already have such a law. The purpose of such legislation is clearly defined as protection of the children, not punishment of the parents. Such legislation constitutes a major step in prevention of child abuse and early identification of abusing families.

Schools also see the results of both neglect and abuse. Alert teachers know when a child is consistently underfed, and comes to school dirty and unkempt. They know, too, when a child shows the marks of a brutal beating. One teacher put her hand lightly on a little boy's shoulder, and he winced in pain.

She sent him to the school nurse who found his back a mass of welts and cuts. Prompt action by the school brought that child to the court's attention. But there are schools that do not want to get involved; one teacher risked her job to make a confidential report to a social agency of an abused child in her classroom.

Social workers may discover child neglect or abuse although the family is known to them for quite different reasons. Their responsibility is clear: to report such situations and to see that protective action is taken.

Identification is only a first step. There needs to be a clear community structure for the reporting of neglecting and abusing families, defined channels of communication that enable responsible citizens to know how and where to take action. Now, complaints may be made to the police, to juvenile authorities, or to child welfare agencies depending on what resource is most familiar to the complainant. There are no standard and clear channels of communication and collaboration between these agencies, and centralization of responsibility with definition of purpose and procedure is rare indeed.

The survey of newspaper-reported cases sponsored by the Children's Division of the American Humane Society learned through investigation that of 434 abuse cases analyzed only 8 had been reported to a social agency. In 3 out of 4 of the families the complaint had been made to the police, sheriff, or juvenile authority. The majority of these complaints had come from a member of the family or a close relative; doctors, hospitals, and neighbors were the next most frequent sources. In this study, nearly all of the complaints of child abuse had been made initially to a child welfare agency and in only a scattering of cases had the police been involved. One reason for the difference is, of course, that the newspapers would be most likely to know about cases that had been reported to the police. Further, the children reported to child welfare tended to be older and in many cases physical injuries were less drastic.

There is considerable argument about who should make the initial investigation of families and whether complaints should be directed primarily to the police or to social agencies. The

question is actually not a simple one. In many abuse cases and
in some neglect cases, the police are better equipped to investigate the immediate situation and take quick action than a
social agency. In more ambiguous circumstances where it may
be difficult to know what is happening behind closed doors, the
child welfare agency may be better able to uncover the facts.
Further, while protection of the children is the primary purpose,
we cannot lose sight of the fact that the murder of a child is a
capital offense even when the murderer is the parent. And investigation of crime is police business.

The most practical solution to this controversy is probably a
special police division, such as already exists in Los Angeles,
that is trained and equipped for this specific responsibility and
that can work in close collaboration with a specific child welfare
agency. Complaints could be made to either and the resources
of both used in the way that offers the maximum protection to
the children. The police are primarily investigatory while the
child welfare agency is concerned with the continuing and long-
range planning and care of the children. Whatever the particular community structure and procedure, there needs to be
centralized responsibility and accountability.

One of the reasons many people hesitate to report cases of
child neglect and abuse is that they fear being involved in
subsequent court action. This is particularly true with child
abuse, where parental opposition and antagonism are likely to
be more violent and where proof of parental behavior may be
more difficult to secure. Social workers are abundantly familiar
with the unhappy person who reports parental abuse of a child
but insists that the report be kept confidential and that he not
be asked to testify—he fears legal reprisal from the parents and
sometimes personal retaliation combined possibly with public
censure.

There have to be procedures which offer reasonable protection to people seeking to protect children. A report of child
neglect or abuse to a responsible agency does not constitute
malicious prying. The family in question has a right to legal
safeguards against this but so have responsible citizens when
they seek to prevent the exploitation of the helpless.

The need for legal clarification in this whole problem is primary. In the United States there has been agitation about brutal parents since the middle of the last century. The first state law that attempted to do something about such parental action was passed in New York as the result of a battle waged by one woman to protect one child. Mrs. Etta Wheeler discovered a little girl who was kept chained to a bedpost, starved, and beaten by her foster mother. When Mrs. Wheeler called the police to protect the child, she learned that there was a law forbidding cruelty to animals but none offering equal protection for children. The child was finally removed from its home on the legal ground that a human being is an animal, and that the law could be stretched to save one small girl.

The reports of the Societies for the Prevention of Cruelty to Children, which came into being about this time, give a vivid picture of certain kinds of family life a hundred years ago. The 1884 report of the Brooklyn Society for the Prevention of Cruelty to Children included cases like these:

DEATH FROM NEGLECT (CASE 4,629)

March 17—A neighbor living at 87 Summit Street called at the Society's office and said that there was a woman in the same house who has a child two years old whom she cruelly neglects, and while the child is sick she leaves it for hours at a time entirely alone, without food or care. He further said that the woman was in the habit of getting drunk frequently, and when remonstrated with threatens to shoot anyone who interferes. Our officer's report of his findings was even worse than the above. The woman's name was Lizzie M——, and her husband, who was an engineer, had not been near here for some time on account of her habits. She had been on a continual spree for some time, and the child, which had been when first seen by the neighbors a healthy, strong child, was now a wasted skeleton, the bones only kept together by the least skin and muscles. The mother, always drunk, rarely in the house except at night, and then not till late, the child had no care or food whatever, except such as the humane neighbors would give it. If the mother came in and found anyone attending to the little sufferer, she would cry out in her drunkenness, "I don't care." "Why, is that child not dead yet?"

The Society in this case was notified too late. Death had already set its seal on little Annie. But all that could be done was at once set in motion. Our Assistant Physician, Dr. Bierwirth, at once visited the house, and on his advice, together with that of Dr. W. A. Northridge, the child was removed to the Long Island College Hospital, but, although all that medical skill and kind, healthful nursing could do was done, little Annie passed away.

What was done to the brute that was responsible for this, you ask? The laws were searched, but sufficient evidence to convict of the gravest offense could not be obtained. Justice F. S. Massey, of the First District Police Court, convicted her of a lesser degree, and sent her to be incarcerated for a year.

UNNATURAL ASSAULT CASE (1,891)

January 8—Few cases have been brought to our attention which have exhibited a more brutal disposition than that of George C——, of Douglass Street. On the above date several of the neighbors rushed into our office with his little girl Katie, and besought the interference of the Society to save this poor little thing, who, though 13 years of age, did not seem to be more than 10. It was charged that although so small, the child was compelled to keep the house, wash the clothes for her father and two grown up brothers, and in other ways was overworked. She had often been seen with black and blue marks on her face and body. The father had recently struck her across the forehead with a cane, blackening both her eyes, and, in fact, the treatment was horrible; the little girl had become somewhat lightheaded. At last one day her father came home and beat her worse than usual, and she, in trying to escape him, ran into the bedroom, and climbing through a small window leading into the hallway, fell to the floor. Here she was picked up by one of the tenants, and afterwards taken out of the house, and the following day brought to our office. This human fiend, her father, was arrested and tried before Justice Bergen, in the First District Police Court, where Assistant District Attorney John F. Clarke prosecuted on behalf of the people.

The little girl's testimony, copied verbatim from the Court notes, was as follows—only such part omitted as we dare not produce here on account of our readers:

"Catherine Cowan, being sworn: I am thirteen and a half years old; defendant is my father—mother is dead; two brothers older than I am in family. On December 24, in evening, my father came in afternoon after dinner; he beat me; he first cursed at me; I had done nothing; he went in bedroom and came out and whipped me with rattan; caught me by hair and struck me five or six times across the back and head; he called me in bedroom after whipping me and wanted me to do something."

CASE (2,776)

March 17—A family named McM——n were found by one of our officers in a cellar without flooring, furniture, fire or food. Four children, between the ages of 4 and 12 years, were vainly striving to keep themselves warm. They had hardly clothing enough on to cover their nakedness, but were covered with vermin and filth. Lying on the ground was the mother in a state of intoxication, while on a half barrel the father, maudlin drunk, tried to tell our officer how hard it was to obtain work. In one corner of this cellar were a large number of chickens and ducks, and in another part two goats were endeavoring to find something to eat in an old tub full to overflowing with filth. Dr. Walker was summoned, who directed how best to make the children comfortable for the night, and the next morning the entire family was taken to Second District Court. The parents were held as vagrants and the children were taken by our Society, cleaned and warmly clothed, after which they were committed to an Institution.

The reports of 1884 talked about "fiends in human form" and the reports of 1963 describe "pathological parents." In these eighty years little seems to have changed in these families except the language by which we describe them. In most states now we have laws against parental neglect and abuse, but they are still not effective.

Most laws are general in their definition of what constitutes parental neglect and abuse, and they are subject to considerable variability in interpretation. What one court considers neglect or abuse may differ from the standard used by another court. There is little uniformity in the kind and extent of evidence required before a judge will take action in a specific case. Social workers are aware that what may be considered by one judge evidence sufficient to warrant removal of a child from his home may be ruled inadequate by another judge. This leaves the most responsible agency without consistent standards and guides in how and when to initiate court action. It also reenforces the reluctance of many social agencies to use the court even when the need is all too evident.

Courts have with justification criticized social agencies for failure to present clear, specific evidence of parental behavior. This only points up, however, the need for a clear and consistent standard of what constitutes competent evidence. Such a standard must take into account the difficulties inherent in securing evidence, particularly in abuse cases. This is not a plea for reducing the standard of evidence required, but for recognition that adequate provision must be made for securing it. Social workers may have real difficulty in securing necessary information when witnesses refuse to testify in court and when social agencies have no legal authority even to enter a home without parental permission. There must be some legal provision for investigating abuse cases in which protection of the children is a vital consideration and in which a lengthy process of observation may be dangerous to the children and discouraging or futile for the people attempting to protect them.

Judge Justine Polier has pointed out one factor in this dilemma when she observes, "Unfortunately, when the matter is brought to Court, whether by police, citizen or social agency, it is brought in as an adversary proceeding for a finding of neglect. Removal of the child is therefore regarded as punishment after a hearing, rather than as a preliminary step to full exploration of what is the best interests of the child." In effect punishment of the parents has too often served to obscure the real need in which courts, agencies, and public should be cooperating: protection of the children.

The emphasis on punishment has also served to promote the practice of temporary removal of children from their natural parents, even when it was clear at the point of placement that parents would never be able to provide even the most minimally adequate home for their children. Children have been removed to "teach the parents a lesson," and the question became, Do the parents deserve a life sentence? instead of, What is right for the children? Many of the parents themselves reflected the punishment motivation when they asked to have their children returned "because we've been punished enough." The real consideration, the welfare of the children, tended to be lost in the conflicting emotions of adults. We cannot at the same time seek to punish and to protect.

Judge Polier has summed up the needs in this situation with great clarity.[1]

Our limited laws vesting powers in the Courts to terminate parental rights, the requirements of evidence that is competent, material and relevant, the attitudes of Judges who respond to emotional appeals to try children out once more with inadequate and disturbed parents, or the feelings of some Judges that it is not for them to sever the "natural ties" between parents and children, all contribute to the problems of freeing children from ties that can never be healthy and of preventing opportunities for new and ongoing relationships.

New legislation may be needed in many jurisdictions to clarify and enlarge the power of the Courts to terminate parental rights where the evidence shows there is no reasonable expectation of a healthy parent-child relationship. Equally important, if not more important, is the imposition by legislation on authorized agencies, including both public and voluntary agencies, of the duty to provide real and not token services to parents as soon as a child is removed, and to submit regular reports to the Courts or public departments responsible for placement as to progress made and as to what they are or are not able to achieve with parents.

Perhaps the most important, if the present tragic picture is to be changed, will be the creation by our communities of far more adequate preventive and protective services to avoid placement, ongoing services immediately following placement, and a very great increase in permanent substitute or adoptive homes for children whose only hope for emotional security lies in such care. In this connection, we must face the discrepancy between what we say about the importance of family life and what the American community is prepared to do to strengthen it. It has always seemed paradoxical that the community under present Federal, State and local laws will do least to maintain a child within his own home and more and more as his placement makes return to normal life

[1]Honorable Justine W. Polier, "Orphans With Parents—Parental Rights in the Law and the Courts" (Unpublished paper).

in the community less and less likely or possible. Thus, we add 60 cents a day as an allowance for an additional child in an ADC home, pay $2 to $3 a day for the same child in a foster home, where we hope to secure far more than physical care, $5 to $7 for the same child in a congregate institution, and from $10 to $12 a day when the child becomes emotionally disturbed and in need of residential treatment and services.

The laws, the practices of agencies, the general confusion reflect the attitude of the public. Are we concerned about these children or only about what they do that causes trouble for the community? Prevention begins before the trouble can happen. Without public knowledge and public responsibility no preventive program can hope to be successful. The philosophy "never get involved" can only leave the problem to fester until it involves even those most assiduous in avoiding it. The isolation of modern urban living is not only an ideal breeding ground of neglect and abuse families but a potent factor in the breakdown of community controls and personal responsibility. One of the striking indications that appeared in this study was the tendency toward much quicker community action in the rural than in the urban areas. There was greater personal knowledge of child neglect and abuse, and there was also greater assumption of personal responsibility to do something about it with the assurance of community approval and support. The larger the city the more difficult such personal knowledge becomes and the weaker the imperative of personal responsibility and action.

This does not mean that the individual citizen is helpless to change great social problems like this one; in fact, only individual citizens can change them. Their understanding of the problem and their awareness of what is happening in their own community is a gigantic first step. What agencies are responsible for meeting this situation? What are the working policies of agencies, courts, professional groups directly involved? Are court calendars so crowded that the most conscientious judge and court staff are helpless to give the attention that should be going into decisions affecting the whole lives of human beings? Are child welfare agencies compelled to send young, untrained caseworkers into homes like these to face situations

that would baffle a Solomon? Are workers asked to supervise
fifty, seventy, a hundred families when to look after fifteen or
twenty would exhaust the most experienced? Are these workers
being asked to face these situations day after day at a salary
that in some communities is less than that of the garbage
collectors?

Any citizen's group can find out with a little effort what is
happening in its own community. The direct responsibility for
protecting children must be delegated to specific agencies,
courts, social agencies, children's hospitals. It is important to
know how well coordinated their responsibilities are, how
effective their policies and resources for meeting present and
future needs are. Does community planning make maximum
use of existing resources so that money is spent to give the
most possible service to children? Does one agency carry the
primary responsibility so that accountability for the welfare of
children is possible?

One reason these questions have not been more generally explored is the fear that to solve them will require the expenditure
of still more tax money. At a time when pressures seem endless
it is easy to look for short cuts and assume that a little old-
fashioned toughness will somehow settle the whole business.
There is at present a wave of wishful thinking that promotes
the attractive idea that if we do nothing about problems they
will solve themselves; abusing and neglecting families will
somehow work out their own difficulties without bothering
other people. It is unfortunate that the idea is often tagged
"realistic."

Actually it is the old longing to have one's cake and eat it
too. The same changes which have brought material prosperity
to many, that have brightened the face of progress, have also
created new problems and made old ones more acute or more
urgent. Thus, we have been wrong in our assumption that social
controls remained adequate, that families either conformed to
them or could easily be made to do so.

Unless pathological families receive continuing and consistent, personalized help they have neither the volition nor
the means to conform to society's norms. People do not spon-

taneously decide one fine Monday morning that they are going to change their way of living, proceed to do so at the price of enormous effort, and then maintain the change, especially when they have neither strength nor incentive and no conviction that it would benefit them much anyway. For people as passive as those in our study the idea that an occasional lecture or threat will accomplish such change is a patent absurdity.

"Closing the case" under these circumstances is no standard of success. It is more likely to be an admission of failure or a temporary resignation from the situation. As a matter of fact, most of the records in this study had been repeatedly opened and closed, some of them eight and ten times, to the destruction of consistent accomplishment of almost any on-going plan for family change. Lack of community understanding has been a potent force in promoting such on-again, off-again assistance which handles the family crisis when it has already occurred and does little or nothing to prevent the next one. Even in economic terms it is the most expensive kind of assistance imaginable. To invest money in helping human beings become productive members of society and then fail to invest the tenacity, thought, and extra money that make results possible is not good economy.

We have to face the fact that there are no quick and easy solutions to the complex social and psychological problems of parent neglect and abuse. We have to explore new ways of meeting them, find new means of providing more effective social controls and of strengthening external supports for families that lack internal stability. While controls from the outside are not the same as cure of the disease and do not obviate the need for learning what are the causes of such social ills, they do have a considerable limiting effect upon the opportunity and freedom of parents to behave in this way. This does not mean that a lecture by the judge, official warnings, or repeated admonitions will do the job. Nor does it mean that punitive actions—cutting families off relief, public humiliation of children and parents, criminal procedures which aim at punishing the parents and forget protection of the children— will be effective. Controls are preventive as well as corrective.

In fact, one of their chief purposes is prevention of undesirable behavior.

Even when families can be helped to live up to the minimal standards of society, these parents will not be able automatically to give to their children warmth and assurance. There is a difference between a structure that stands and the contents of its rooms. In many, if not most, of the families, children will need help in reaching groups to which they can really belong, in finding new opportunities, in developing interests and talents, and hopefully in finding and making genuine friends. Probably none of these can totally compensate for what their families could not give, but children, if we help them before too much damage is done, can thrive and grow on all kinds of help. The churches, too, could do a major job in helping these children grow roots in a way of life different than that their parents knew.

The need for child protection is nothing new in human history. What is different now is our knowledge about it—meager as that still is—and the degree of its importance to our demanding, fast-moving society in a time that needs strong, mature people as perhaps never before. The passive dependence of the neglecting families and the destructiveness of the abusing families represent not only personal tragedies but areas of major weakness in our society. Many of them belong to that two-fifths of our population who still live in poverty or deprivation. We might prefer not to look at problems so grim—particularly when every new change of our time seems to swell that wave of social ills—but we cannot turn away for long. We need to look, and we need to re-orient our thinking, and we need to begin to understand.

We need to bring order into the flood of social ills and to discriminate between the basic ills and their diverse consequences. We have to surrender the cheerful illusion that seriously pathological people are quickly and cheaply cured. The suggestions made in this chapter for helping those families that can be stabilized aim at reaching and holding minimal standards, not at cure of their pathology. If we have made it possible for their grandchildren to be strong and mature, we have given mighty service to the future. In our anxiety to strengthen and revitalize that most important of all human institutions, the family, we need to distinguish between what is truly a family and what one astute social worker calls the "phantom family." Keeping people together under one roof is not the same as maintaining the family. Actually, we are weakening the family and undermining its great purpose when we permit thousands of children to grow up with no other experience of family living than that of abuse or neglect. We need to reforge the bond between parental responsibilities and parental rights, and we need to implement the protection of discipline and forego the impulse to punish.

In concrete steps of planning we need to think always of prevention, even as we struggle with the crises of correction. We need new and better legislation that uses the knowledge we have to protect children, not to punish parents. We need community planning specifically devised to make the best use possible of every available dollar, to give the maximum benefit to children, and to coordinate and develop every potential resource to its fullest capacity. We need greater public understanding of the problems and complexities child welfare faces in trying to protect children and greater support of its efforts and needs. In response we need greater professional accountability to that public understanding and support.

Finally, we need much more knowledge. We need the steady, continuing collection of disciplined observations that child welfare could with thought and purpose contribute from all over the nation. We need research that will pursue the many questions that can only be suggested by this study. We need to know causes and means and fulfillable goals. We need the discipline of patience and persistence as we try to learn. The solutions to the problems of the human heart are not found. They are grown.

Appendix

METHOD OF STUDY *Selection of Sample*

The exploratory study included the analysis of 120 case records, selected from 3 agencies. Two of them were public child welfare agencies suburban to a large eastern city, and the third was a specifically protective agency located in this city. All records were selected, by the judgment of professionally trained supervisors, as representative of the total group of such families coming to their agency.

The items covered in the schedule used in the second part of the study were abstracted from the findings of the prior exploratory project. One hundred and eighty cases were analyzed, using this schedule. Forty-seven were selected from the public Child Welfare Department of a medium-sized Midwestern city, and 11 from a small Midwestern city. Thirty-three came from the rural area of a Midwestern state, 39 from a private protective agency in a large metropolitan area in the Midwest, 29 from a medium size city in the Northwest, and 21 from a rural area in the Northwest.

The rationale for the geographical sampling was twofold. First, it seemed important to determine whether there were any significant differences between families living in rural areas and small towns, and those in medium and large urban centers. Secondly, the geographical diversity should serve to minimize the influence of possible regional factors, such as one specific cultural group or an atypical community attitude. It had been hoped that a larger number of completely rural cases could be used, but the difficulty in locating such cases with sufficiently complete information made this too time-consuming to be practicable.

In all but three of the agencies, the cases were selected by the judgments of the responsible supervisors. They were asked to choose the cases (1) according to the complaint criterion, (2) those that in their best judgment were representative of all the protective cases coming to them, and (3) those that were most complete in information recorded. It was necessary to select cases by the judgments of the supervisors, since protective cases were not separated statistically from the total caseload and were not identified as such. In order to eliminate this factor of judgment, it was planned in the voluntary, protective agency to select all cases by random sampling. This was possible here since the community complaint constituted the basis of referral of families to the agency. This was found to be feasible only with the neglect complaints, since the agency had a policy of referring severe abuse cases directly to the juvenile court, and carried only a small proportion of the abuse complaints. The supervisor was asked to select abuse cases carried by the agency, since the random sample would otherwise have been heavily biased in the direction of neglecting parents. These abuse cases are necessarily biased in the direction of the less severe and less urgent. For the rest, every fifth record from the active caseload was pulled until a sample of 20 was secured.

In the Northwestern city, the supervisor of the county child welfare department was asked to select 12 protective cases. Then 17 more were pulled as a random sample, every tenth case from the active caseload. In the rural Northwestern area, all the cases were selected at random. Every tenth record in the active child welfare caseload was pulled until a sample of 22 was secured. It was hoped to use these cases as a comparison sample with those that had been selected by the complaint criterion. This would obviously not constitute a comparison with so-called normal families, since all these families had some problem which had brought them to the child welfare department. However, the assumption was that there would be a variety of problems in the random sample and that many of the families would have come voluntarily to the agency. Also, the percentage of complaint cases in the sample would give some indication of what proportion they represented to the total child welfare caseload of the agency.

TESTING OF THE SCHEDULE

A fifteen-page schedule was devised covering a wide range of information, but with items made as specific as possible. The items were designed to elicit information in accordance with the propositions abstracted from the prior study. Such information as marital status, income level, education and housing was recorded as of the beginning of the agency contact, though any later changes were noted on the back of the schedule.

All but one of the items (that one asked for parental statements) were phrased in dichotomous form, that is, to be answered as true or false. Items were marked true or false when the observations in the record were deemed sufficient to warrant the conclusion. These observations might be a doctor's report that a child was seriously undernourished, or repeated recording by the caseworkers of certain kinds of parental behavior, as lack of cleanliness or physical abuse of children, or reports of specific parental behavior coming from several different sources, as school, neighbors, relatives. The conclusions frequently involved judgments on the part of the case reader, but here expert judgment based on the recorded behavior of the family was used as the determinant. Since such items as attitude toward placement and the demonstration of parental guilt about behavior are necessarily general and often ambiguous, an attempt was made to break down these items into specific and observable indices. These indices are, of course, arbitrary, and the author makes no claim that they are either exhaustive or conclusive. While any one of them singly might well be inaccurate as an index, taken collectively they represent a distillation of experience that it is hoped provides them with some validity and points the way toward a more definitive structuring of indices. Those devised here do not by any means obviate subjective judgment, but do attempt to circumscribe it and provide more explicit bases for it.

While it may be argued that the phrasing of the items in

dichotomous form introduces a measure of error by making them arbitrary, it was hoped that this would be counterbalanced by the greater precision possible both in the structuring and analyzing of the observations. Further, the schedule allowed for two quantitative categories in describing behavior, consistent and sporadic.

The schedule was pretested on 3 records, which were read independently by 3 case readers. Comparison of result indicated ambiguity in a number of the items and these were clarified. An additional factor of importance became apparent as a result of the pretesting. There was a clear tendency to bias judgment of what happened in terms of why it happened. In other words, observation of behavior was influenced by factors which in the reader's judgment caused the behavior. Once this became clear, there was agreement on the observations of behavior. This pointed up a real danger, against which the 2 case readers on the study itself took particular precautions. Space was allowed in the final schedule form for qualifying remarks which might illumine or explain particular observations, but only the behavior itself was recorded in answer to specific items.

The revised schedule was again tested on 5 records by the author and the case reader who assisted on the study. This time there was a high degree of consistency when the results were compared and minor confusions were eliminated.

METHOD OF ANALYSIS

Data from the first 3 pages of the schedule covered a variety of information, economic, educational, medical and social, about the family. These were tabulated by subject. They were not correlated case by case with the rest of the data, as was done with the main body of the material. This would have been extremely time-consuming, and there was no evidence in the data that it would have yielded results sufficiently significant to warrant such an expenditure.[1] However, the cases were separated according to geography.

The rest of the data was analyzed on a case-by-case basis. All

[1]These variables were not controlled for this study and they represent descriptive background for the patterns of family interaction and behavior.

cases were separated according to geography. Both neglect and abuse cases were divided into 2 categories—severe and moderate.

For the analysis, 173 cases were used. Seven cases showed neither parental neglect nor abuse and were a part of the sample of 38 cases that had been randomly selected. Since the number was too small to use as a comparison sample, they were omitted. The 173 cases were divided into the 4 types, according to the arbitrary criteria specified.

The 95 items in the schedule were tabulated by the responses true, false and no information. These responses described the presence or absence in the family of the behavior specified by the item. When an item referred to repetitive behavior, the predominant trend of such behavior determined the nature of the response. When more than 50 percent of the cases showed no information on a specific item, that item was not used. There were eleven such items.

Percentages of true and false responses were figured for each of the remaining 84 items. The hypothesis that the classifications true and false on any item were independent of type was made. The chi-square test was applied and only those items for which this hypothesis could be rejected were retained. The purpose of this was to determine whether type, as defined by the criteria, was a significant variable in delineating specific family behavioral patterns.

Chi-square tables (2×4) were constructed for each item. Chi-square tests were made on 53 items. Thirty-seven of these proved to be significantly related to type at a level of .05 or below. The nature of this relationship and the relationships among the items as applied to behavioral patterns were analyzed by their empirical meaning and logical consistency. On 31 items expected frequencies were too low for a chi-square test to be made, since the pattern of responses was relatively the same for all groups. Fifteen items out of the 47 that failed to show any significant relationship to type were analyzed and discussed in a separate chapter because the percentage of true responses showed them to be of major importance for the total group. While they were not differentiating items for this sample, they might be sharply distinguishing ones in a comparison with a sample of less disorganized families. They are of practical importance for social work practice, since they are present in so large a percentage of the families.

This process has been used as a means of abstracting the broad outlines of family behavioral patterns, as a first step in constructing the typologies that may later be tested on a different sample and that may then be more precisely refined. While every effort was made to confine items to visible behavior, there was inevitably a considerable degree of subjective judgment involved in the determination of responses within such arbitrary limits as true and false. Further, many items did not indicate degree of behavior or in some cases precise nature of parental action. It is almost inevitable that some distortion and confusion have as a result been introduced into the behavioral profiles. Yet for the purpose of this study this represents a lesser danger than the attempt to achieve greater refinement and precision prematurely. It is the broad perspective and inclusiveness that are important at this point, even though the findings must as a consequence be regarded as tentative and hypothetical.

SIGNIFICANT ITEMS IN THE BEHAVIORAL
SYNDROME OF PARENTS

Thirty-seven items showed a significant relationship to the 4 typologies that had been arbitrarily determined by the stated criteria. Nineteen of these were significant at the .001 level, 11 at the .01 level, 3 at the .02 level and 4 at the .05 level. On the basis of their empirical meaning, the items fell into 3 main divisions, Parental Behavior Toward Children, Marital Roles and Family Standards of Behavior.

There are 19 distinguishing items in the first division, which is related to parental treatment of children. The table on the following pages lists these items and gives the percentage of true responses and the chi-squares.

All of these items concern physical neglect or abuse. "Inadequate feeding was, of course, the determining criterion for defining severe neglect and therefore appeared in 100% of the severe neglect cases. It was important for the other 3 groups, but to a considerably lesser extent. It appeared in 65.1% of the severe abuse families and in 61.8% of the moderate abuse. It was conspicuously less in moderate neglect, 40.6%.

It would be difficult to exaggerate the importance of this item. While it was in this study impossible to define precise degrees of inadequacy, it always described consistent under-feeding severe enough to be visible to outsiders. Its prevalence in the abuse cases and the relatively small difference between severe and moderate abuse are noteworthy. It is possible that inadequate feeding in these families has a punitive connotation.

"Severe beating" was, of course, by definition present in all severe abuse cases, and in less severe and consistent form was true of 72% of the families in the moderate abuse group. It was arbitrarily excluded from severe and moderate neglect. Associated with this item, however, were the "presence of physical torture," "the consistent denial of normal activities to the children," and "negative verbal statements of feeling about the children." "Abusive language," while a less sharply differentiating item, properly belongs with the behavioral constellation. Physical torture of the children was present in 69.7% of the families in severe abuse, but in only 25% of the families in moderate abuse.

While behavior so drastic as physical torture would seem to belong entirely in severe abuse, the data indicated that it occurred in less extreme form in the moderate abuse group and was not often repeated. The records noted that behavior of this kind, such as slamming a child against a wall or kicking him, had occurred at least once, but this was often the only recorded mention of it. It was noted on the schedule as sporadic behavior. It appeared in .02% (1 family) of the cases in severe neglect, and not at all in moderate neglect. In other words, parental torturing of children was confined to the abusing groups, and there was a conspicuous difference between severe and moderate abuse. It should be noted that this item was not used in the original definitions of the abuse categories. This would seem to indicate that, wherever even isolated physical torture of a child is found, it can be expected that the child is also subjected to severe beatings at least sporadically.

SIGNIFICANT ITEMS CONCERNING
PARENTAL BEHAVIOR TOWARD CHILDREN

d.f. = 3 Items	Severe Abuse		Moderate Abuse		Severe Neglect		Moderate Neglect		X^2	P
	Total N	% True	Total N	% True	Total N	% True	Total N	% True		
Severe beating with other than hand	43	100.0	33	72.0	58	0.0	31	0.0	138.1	.001
Physical torture	43	69.7	32	25.0	58	0.02	32	0.0	76.1	.001
Consistent denial of normally accepted activities	42	69.0	32	56.3	60	10.0	29	10.3	52.4	.001
Inadequate feeding	43	65.1	34	61.8	63	100.0	32	40.6	43.5	.001
Negative verbal statements of feeling for children	41	82.9	31	54.8	52	40.4	32	21.9	30.0	.001
Lack of cleanliness	42	52.4	34	61.8	63	95.2	33	69.7	27.4	.001
Inadequate clothing	41	61.0	34	64.7	62	98.4	33	63.6	27.2	.001
Refusal to let child attach himself to anyone else	41	58.5	33	27.3	62	16.1	32	15.6	25.4	.001
Abusive language	39	94.9	32	71.9	55	54.5	30	50.0	21.9	.001
Positive verbal statements of feeling for children	41	26.8	31	58.1	51	68.6	32	59.4	17.3	.001

SIGNIFICANT ITEMS CONCERNING
PARENTAL BEHAVIOR TOWARD CHILDREN

d.f. = 3 Items	Severe Abuse		Moderate Abuse		Severe Neglect		Moderate Neglect		X^2	P
	Total N	% True	Total N	% True	Total N	% True	Total N	% True		
Refusal to cooperate with anyone else in care of child	43	83.7	34	73.5	63	61.9	32	40.6	16.5	.001
Slapping and hitting with hand	42	83.3	28	71.4	53	47.2	25	56.0	16.0	.01
Failure to give needed medical care	41	75.6	32	65.6	62	95.2	31	71.0	15.2	.01
Leaves children alone for hours	43	27.9	33	48.5	62	64.5	32	43.8	14.0	.01
Leaves children alone for days	43	4.7	33	9.1	62	29.0	33	15.2	12.9	.01
Hostile and refusing to placement of children	40	60.0	31	41.9	57	26.3	25	32.0	11.9	.01
Refusal of help for child	42	66.7	34	50.0	62	43.6	32	31.3	9.9	.01
Willing for placement of children	40	42.5	31	61.3	58	69.0	25	48.0	7.9	.05
Nagging and scolding	43	81.4	29	69.0	52	54.3	29	55.2	7.8	.05

"Physical torture" was differentiated from "severe beating with other than hand" because the specific nature of it illuminated the parental behavior further and because it eliminated the possibility of impulsive rage. It is possible for a parent to beat a child in a rage, but it seems highly unlikely that this would hold true for physical torture. This item covered such behavior as bending back a child's fingers, twisting a child's arm until it broke, kicking, biting, scratching and burning children. This behavior is so extreme that it is difficult to see how it can bear any relation to discipline or to parental punishment of children in the usual sense. These were the children hospitalized for their injuries, frequently for broken bones and severe burns.

A similar pattern of difference appeared with the item of "consistent denial of normally accepted activities" to children. This denial appeared in 69% of the families in severe abuse, 56.3% of those in moderate abuse, in 10% of the families in severe neglect, and in 10.3% of those in moderate neglect.

"Consistent denial of normally accepted activities" covered parental refusal to permit children the usual recreational and educational opportunities open to the other children in that community or in that particular economic level. Thus, school activities which might involve organized sports, parties or something as simple as playing in a neighborhood group after school were forbidden by these parents to their children. Participation in formal and informal neighborhood activities were denied. These children had often to be home from school at a specific moment, and any delay—even so slight a one as that occasioned by a casual, impromptu bit of conversation—was dangerous to them. The ordinary course of childhood friendships was impossible for them, as were any meaningful contacts with adults outside the home. Opportunities for the expression of individual interests or of the curiosity normal for any child, or for the explorations and private projects that are usually a part of the experienced learning of childhood were denied. The children in these families were as a result seriously deprived of contacts and experiences which could offer them any firsthand knowledge of a way of life different from that in their own families.

This deliberate deprivation has to be distinguished from that of the neglected children, even though the end results seem so similar. Children from neglecting but not abusing families were often ostracized by other children and excluded from their activities, but this was not the result of parental prohibition. It could accurately be described as parental responsibility since the physical neglect precipitated the social exclusion, but this was not the overt intent of the parents. It was a consequence of what they did not do, while with the abusing parents it was the ordered consequence. While the results were damaging for both groups of children, there is a considerable psychological difference between the two situations. Further, the children of neglecting families were not deprived of their freedom and their chance for other contacts in the same way nor to the same degree as those from abusing families.

The item "negative verbal statements of feeling for children" referred to gross parental expressions of hostility and aggression. Parents stated bluntly that they hated the children. Some expressed an open wish to kill them or a hope that they would die. Others remarked that they had never liked them, had never wanted them. A parent referred frequently to his son as "crazy," the "idiot," or a child was repeatedly told he was "dumb." In other cases a parent emphasized how physically ugly a child was or called him the "criminal." These statements were made both to the caseworker and to the other person in the presence of the children. They revealed an indifference to the reactions of either children or adult listeners. This kind of parental behavior was true of 82.9% of the families in severe abuse, 54.8% of those in moderate abuse. It existed in 40.4% of the severe neglect cases and in 21.9% of those in moderate neglect.

"Abusive language" referred to a consistent yelling at children in profane and vulgar terms. Name calling, insulting phrases, crude mockery were common. This kind of parental behavior was present in 94.9% of the families in severe abuse, in 71.9% of those in moderate abuse. It was true of 54.5% of the severe neglect cases and of 50% of the moderate neglect.

The behavior outlined by these items is sharply differentiated by type. Severely abusing families in this study both feed their children inadequately and abuse them physically. Severely neglecting families feed their children inadequately, but there is virtually no physical abuse. A very small percentage of them deny normal activities and opportunities to their children, and a larger number express verbal hostility and aggression. Moderate abuse families show the same pattern as severe abuse but in considerably lesser degree. Moderate neglect follows the same pattern as severe neglect, except again in lesser degree. It would be interesting to know whether neglecting families that deprive their children of normal activities do so for different motivations than abusing parents. Since this study concentrated on visible behavior, it is not possible to answer that.

Interestingly the item "positive statements of feeling for children" showed less variation than its opposite. It followed the same pattern in that it was least likely to be present in severe abuse families. This described parental statements that praised the children, gave some indication of concern, expressed some pride in them. It was true in 68.6% of the severe neglect families and rather surprisingly in only 59.4% of the moderate neglect. Moderate abuse families were on this item almost identical with moderate neglect, 58.1%, while severe abuse diverged sharply, with only 26.8% of the families showing any such behavior.

Severe neglect families were consistently the highest of all the groups in extent of physical neglect of the children. Associated with inadequate feeding were lack of cleanliness, lack of medical care, inadequate clothing of children. They left children alone more often, sometimes for days. Except for inadequate feeding, the most clearly differentiating items of physical neglect were "lack of cleanliness" and "inadequate clothing." Lack of cleanliness referred to a consistent condition of dirtiness that attracted attention to the children and represented both a health hazard and a social handicap. The baby who could not move his fingers because they were so encrusted with dirt and the family who used the middle of the floor for garbage are examples of the extent of filthiness that could be found at the more extreme degree. At no time did this item apply to what might be called normal dirtiness, that is, children playing outside, temporary disruptions of household practice or disorderliness as such. Usually complaints from school and neighbors supplemented the observations of the caseworkers. It was true of 95.2% of the families in severe neglect, 69.7% of those in moderate neglect, 52.4% of the cases in severe abuse and 61.8% of those in moderate abuse.

"Inadequate clothing" described parental indifference to the way children were dressed. Many children, for example, went to school in clothes that were torn, or that had belonged to an adult and were highly inappropriate to them. Small children were often left to run about the home with little or no clothing, even in cold weather. At no time was this item used to denote economic inability to provide more adequate clothing. While the families were usually poor, resources to clothe the children more decently were available to them. As a matter of fact, in most of these cases clothing had been provided by some outside source, but this had little or no effect upon the way the children were dressed. This was true of 98.4% of the severe neglect families, of 63.6% of moderate neglect, of 61% of severe abuse cases and of 64.7% of moderate abuse.

Both of these items trace an interesting pattern, at variance both with inadequate feeding and with abusing behavior. There is a steady reduction in degree, with severe neglect at the top, moderate neglect and moderate abuse at a roughly similar level, and severe abuse at the bottom, showing the least neglect in these areas.

"Failure to provide needed medical care" for children was again most often true in the severe neglect group, 95.2% of the families. Severe abuse was next highest, however, with 75.6% of the cases showing this kind of neglect. Moderate neglect and moderate abuse families were roughly similar, with moderate neglect showing 71% and moderate abuse 65.6%.

"Leaving children alone for hours" and "leaving children alone for days" are related items of physical neglect. They described a continuing pattern of parental behavior, under circumstances where there was no rational necessity for leaving children unprotected and where their age required adult supervision. It did not refer to crisis situations where parents had no alternative, nor to single atypical incidents. In the severe neglect group, 64.5% of the families left children alone for hours and 29% of them for more than a day at a time. In the moderate neglect group, 43.8% of the families left children alone for hours and 15.2% of them for more than a day. Families of the severe abuse type left children alone for hours in 27.9% of the cases and for days in 4.7% of the total number. Moderate abuse families left children alone for hours in 48.5% of the cases and for days in 9.1%. On both these items, severe neglect rated highest and severe abuse lowest. Moderate neglect and moderate abuse were again closer to each other. This is much the same pattern as was true of "lack of cleanliness" and "inadequate clothing."

"Slapping and hitting with hand" and "nagging and scolding" are behaviors which are punitive but not necessarily abusive. They both, however, showed differentiation among the types. Slapping and hitting occurred in 83.3% of the severe abuse families and in 71.4% of the moderate abuse. It was true of only 47.2% of severe neglect and of 56% of moderate neglect. Nagging and scolding were true of 81.4% of the severe abuse families and of 69% of the moderate abuse. They occurred in 54.3% of the severe neglect cases and in 55.2% of moderate neglect. While they show much less variation in degree than the truly abuse items, they follow substantially the same pattern. It would be interesting to know whether the higher percentage of slapping and scolding in the moderate neglect group as compared with that in severe neglect is indicative of a greater degree of discipline by moderate neglect parents. In other words, is this normal parental punishment connected with specific offenses of the children and consistent in its enforcement of specific rules?

Parental behavior characterized by these items of physical neglect outlines a consistent pattern, in which severe neglect families show the highest incidence of such behavior and severe abuse the lowest. Moderate neglect and moderate abuse tend to be considerably more similar. Slapping and scolding follow more closely the pattern of abusive behavior.

The remaining 5 items in this section describe parental behavior toward outside intervention, usually agency, that strives to help the children directly. As such, that behavior is indicative of parental attitudes toward the children as well as their attitudes toward official intervention.

"Refusal to let a child attach himself to anyone else" referred to a parental ban on friendships or close personal relationships between a child and anyone outside the immediate family. In most cases, this outside person was an adult, a caseworker or a teacher. The records did not often indicate whether a child attempted to form such a friendship with another child, and the likelihood is that this did not often occur under the family circumstances of most of these children. It appeared most frequently when a caseworker or a teacher took a special interest in a particular child and offered that child personal attention and help. Thus, a caseworker might try to see the child apart from the family or take him on recreational outings, or a teacher might make a special effort to include a child in school activities or talk with him individually.

Of the severe abuse families, 58.5% refused to permit such attachments. In the moderate abuse group, 27.3% refused. Among the neglecting families, 16.1% of severe neglect and 15.6% of moderate neglect refused. The severe abuse type was conspicuously different in this behavior from the neglecting groups, and moderate abuse—while higher on this item than neglecting families—was considerably lower than severe abuse.

"Parental refusal to cooperate with anyone else in the care of the child" referred to those situations in which an outside agency planned specific care for a child and asked for parental assistance. A social agency might arrange for medical care at a clinic and ask that a parent take the child to the clinic. A caseworker might arrange appointments for a child in the agency office and ask that a parent arrange to send him to the office. Since the needs of most of these children were acute, this tended to be a recurrent situation.

Of the severe abuse group, 83.7% of the families refused, and 73.5% of the moderate abuse families denied parental assistance. In the neglecting families, 61.9% of severe neglect and 40.6% of moderate neglect were unwilling to give parental cooperation. Again, there is a conspicuous difference between abusing and neglecting families. There is a steady reduc-

tion in the parental refusal of assistance, with severe abuse at
the top and moderate neglect at the bottom. Less than half
of the moderate neglect parents refused to cooperate with
outside help.

"Refusal of help for a child" described situations in which
parents openly refused to permit some kind of assistance offered
by an outside person or agency. A casework agency might offer
to send the children to camp or to arrange membership for
them in a neighborhood program or settlement house. Unlike
the previous item, the parents refused the offer itself, not simply
their participation in it. While parental refusal to cooperate
might be simply a more bland way of refusing the proffered
help, there is clearly a difference in the action itself.

In the abusing families, 66.7% of severe abuse and 50.0% of
moderate abuse refused such help. In the neglecting families,
43.6% of severe neglect and 31.3% of moderate neglect refused. The same pattern of steady reduction of parental unwillingness from severe abuse to moderate neglect holds true,
with the difference that less than half of severe neglect refused
outside help for their children.

Parental attitude toward placement of the children outside
of the home was, of course, relevant only when the question
was raised by an agency or by the court. When an agency con-
cluded that children should be removed from the home, or
considered it a sufficiently valid plan to warrant serious discussion with the parents, the parental reaction was clear and overt.
Two responses were predominant. One group of parents was
"hostile and refusing to placement of children." They not only
opposed the idea of placement but were aggressively antagonistic to the agency. In this group fell 60.0% of the severe
abuse families and 41.9% of the moderate abuse. Among the
neglecting families, 26.3% of severe neglect and 32.0% of the
moderate neglect reacted with hostile refusal.

The other parental response was exactly opposite and indicated "willingness to place the children." These parents expressed such willingness either directly in words or indirectly
in behavior which precipitated such outside action, accompanied by passive acquiescence in it. This was true of 42.5% of

the families in the severe abuse type and of 61.3% of the families in moderate abuse. Among the neglecting families it was true of 69.0% of severe neglect and 48.0% of moderate neglect. Both severe abuse and moderate neglect families were similar in their responses to this item, and it is unfortunate that the item cannot differentiate or elucidate their motivations. It seems likely that parents in these 2 groups would differ in their reasons for their consent to placements. The same question would have to be raised in relation to the similarity of response between moderate abuse and severe neglect.

The percentage disparities in the abuse groups were the result of confusion in two or three cases, where both responses were seemingly true at different times in the case histories. In other words, a parent expressed willingness at one point and hostility at another. This contradiction is probably more seeming than real and may be a response to community pressure at a given point, rather than indicative of a continuing attitude. The families in the neglect groups not responding to either of these items were classified under other qualifying items, included in the unit of items concerned with parental attitude toward placement. With these items it must also be noted that the response of the parents may have been influenced by the approach of the agency to them and by their attitude toward the caseworker who initiated the discussion. While the nature of such influence cannot be determined here, the data indicated that, when parents had a good relationship with the caseworker, they were more willing to accept the placement plan.

The second general division concerns marital roles. There were 9 significant items which distinguished among the types. The table on the following page lists these items and gives the percentage of true responses and the chi-squares.

The item "parents have defined responsibilities" described consistent activities accepted and acted as family obligations. Normally these activities are an essential part of the orderly running of any family. A father works, takes care of household repairs. A mother cooks, maintains the upkeep of the home. The presence of such defined responsibilities was true of 32.6% of the families in severe abuse, of 20.7% of those in moderate

SIGNIFICANT ITEMS CONCERNING
MARITAL ROLES

d.f. = 3 Items	Severe Abuse		Moderate Abuse		Severe Neglect		Moderate Neglect		X^2	P
	Total N	% True	Total N	% True	Total N	% True	Total N	% True		
Parents have defined responsibilities	43	32.6	29	20.7	62	19.4	31	67.7	24.6	.001
One parent imposes controls	43	60.5	32	37.5	63	19.0	33	57.6	23.3	.001
One parent plans use of money	39	59.0	32	56.3	61	24.6	31	71.0	22.7	.001
Neither parent imposes controls	43	39.5	33	60.6	63	77.8	33	45.5	16.7	.001
Neither parent plans use of money	41	43.9	32	43.8	61	72.1	31	32.3	16.7	.001
One parent makes all or most decisions	43	62.8	32	65.6	63	30.2	33	57.6	16.6	.001
One parent carries all or most responsibilities	43	27.9	32	28.2	63	20.6	32	56.3	13.1	.01
Neither parent takes responsibility for decisions	41	87.8	32	68.8	63	81.0	33	54.5	12.9	.01
Infidelity	32	50.0	24	45.8	52	68.8	24	50.0	7.8	.05

abuse, of 19.4% of the families in severe neglect and of 67.7% of those in moderate neglect. The high percentage in moderate neglect is outstanding and is one of the important indications of the greater degree of family organization in this group. In none of the other types does this appear as a predominant behavior, although severe abuse is higher than the other two. It is interesting that in this area moderate abuse shows about the same degree of disorganization as severe neglect.

Four items concerned the dominance of one parent in family activities. "One parent imposes controls" referred to the restrictions imposed upon children and upon occasion the other parent, as well as upon family activities as a whole. The parent might be father or mother. This was true of 60.5% of the severe abuse families, of 37.5% of the moderate abuse families, of 19.0% of severe neglect and 57.6% of moderate neglect. The similarity between severe abuse and moderate neglect is interesting and illuminating. The item did not, of course, define the nature of the controls, and the difference between the two groups probably lies here. A relatively small percentage of the severe abuse parents had consistent and defined responsibilities, and this would indicate that the parental controls tended to be separate from parental responsibilities. The reverse would appear to be true of moderate neglect. Since controls without the circumscribing limits of responsibility lead to confusion and often to tyrannical conduct, this is an important index for the severe abuse group. Severe neglect families were low on this item, as would be expected. Moderate abuse families showed again a considerably lesser degree of the severe abuse behavior.

"One parent plans use of money" described whether one parent made the decisions as to ways money was spent. It did not evaluate whether such planning was consistent or realistic. The item was true in 59.0% of the severe abuse families and of 56.3% of moderate abuse. It was present in 24.6% of the severe neglect families and in 71.0% of moderate neglect. Again the severe abuse and moderate neglect groups show the highest ratio of this behavior, and again the nature of the planning would be of great importance in assessing the result. Related to defined parental responsibilities, this item would seem to substantiate the greater extent of family organization in the moderate neglect group. Divorced from defined responsibility, it could indicate unrealistic and inconsistent decisions on the use of money.

The third item "one parent makes all or most decisions" referred to the range of everyday decisions affecting the family. It did not evaluate the nature of those decisions nor their consistency, nor did it imply that the parent was responsible in relation to them. It was true of 62.8% of the severe abuse families and of 65.6% of moderate abuse. Among neglecting families, it was true of 30.2% of severe neglect and 57.6% of moderate neglect.

The fourth item "one parent carries all or most responsibilities" is properly an accompanying one to the item on parental decisions. Decisions without a concomitant responsibility must represent very different results for a family. The item was true for 27.9% of the families in severe abuse and of 28.2% of moderate abuse. It was present in 20.6% of the severe neglect families and in 56.3% of moderate neglect. The high percentage of decisions by one parent in the severe and moderate abuse families was accompanied by a low percentage of responsibility carried by one parent. In the severe neglect group, both decisions and responsibilities were carried by one parent in only a minority of the cases. In moderate neglect, both decisions and responsibilities were carried by one parent in a majority of the cases. Together these 4 items highlight the confusion in severe neglect families, the separation of authority and responsibility in the abuse families, and the greater extent of organization in the moderate neglect group. In all this behavior concerned with the dominance of one parent, the data gave no indication that the sex of the dominant parent was consistent. It might be either father or mother, and there appeared to be no predominance by sex.

Three items referred to a lack of family roles fulfilled by the parents. "Neither parent imposes controls" was the first of these. It was true of 39.5% of the families in severe abuse, of 60.6% of those in moderate abuse, of 77.8% of families in severe neglect and of 45.5% of those in moderate neglect. The second item "neither parent plans use of money" was true for 43.9% of the severe abuse families, of 43.8% of moderate abuse, of 72.1% of the severe neglect families and of 32.3% of moderate neglect. The third item "neither parent takes responsibility for decisions" was true for 87.8% of the families in severe abuse, for 68.8% of those in moderate abuse, for 81.0% of families in severe neglect and 54.5% of those in moderate neglect. This item referred specifically to parental responsibility for decisions made by the parent. It was particularly noteworthy in the severe abuse group that the parent making the decisions shifted the responsibility for those decisions under external stress to someone else, often the other parent. Since the other parent neither made the decision nor accepted the responsibility, the result was again chaos. It is not clear why a somewhat similar result appears in the moderate neglect group. Clarification as to the nature of these parental decisions and of the situations in which the parent refused responsibility for them is clearly important.

When these items are considered in relation to each other, certain patterns emerge. Severe abuse families show the lowest ratio of those where neither parent impose controls, the lowest where neither parent plans use of money, and the highest where neither parent takes the responsibility for the decisions. Moderate neglect families show the next lowest ratio of those where neither parent imposes controls, are approximately the same as severe abuse in the item of neither parent planning use of money, and the lowest of all the groups in the ratio of those where neither parent took responsibility. Severe neglect followed a consistent pattern with the highest ratio of parental failure to impose controls or plan use of money, but it was not quite as high as severe abuse in parental failure to take responsibility for decisions. The moderate abuse group showed a high ratio of parental failure to impose controls, next to that of severe neglect, approximately the same ratio as severe abuse and moderate neglect in failure to plan use of money, and fell between severe and moderate neglect in parental failure to take responsibility.

In other words, the severe abuse families show the same pattern of controls and decisions divorced from parental responsibility. Severe neglect families show a pattern of general confusion with parents neither imposing controls, planning money nor taking responsibility. Moderate neglect families show the highest degree of family organization, with a majority where at least one parent makes decisions, and with almost half where at least one parent carries responsibility for them. Moderate abuse families show features of both abuse and neglect types. In more than half of the cases, neither parent imposed family controls; in more than half, however, at least one parent planned use of money, and in almost 70% neither parent took responsibility.

The final item in this division concerned with marital roles was the "presence of infidelity" by one or both partners. This might refer to a single instance, but in most families where it was true it tended to indicate promiscuous behavior. It was true in 50.0% of the severe abuse families and in 45.8% of moderate abuse. It occurred in 68.8% of the severe neglect families and in 50.0% of moderate neglect. Except in severe neglect families, where it would seem to reflect the general family disorganization, there is a surprising similarity in the proportion of infidelity among the groups. It occurred in roughly half the families. The data added a further observation to this. In abusing families, the aggressive partner tended to be the one sexually unfaithful. There was also a rough impression that promiscuity was more frequent in neglecting than abusing families.

The third division of items is concerned with standards of behavior as these applied to parental behavior and attitudes and to family care. There are 9 items that may be rather generally grouped under this heading. The following table lists these items and gives the percentage of true responses, and the chi-squares.

Perhaps the most important of these items is "family routine is present." Family routine was defined as habitual and orderly ways of caring for the family members and the house. It involved such factors as a customary time for meals, meals eaten together by the family, some kind of schedule for cleaning, a customary bedtime for children. In brief, routine represented the organization of the household, a standard of order for day-by-day living. It was present in 40.5% of the severe abuse families, in 21.9% of the moderate abuse families, in 4.8% of the severe neglect families and in 39.4% of moderate neglect.

d.f. = 3 Items	Severe Abuse		Moderate Abuse		Severe Neglect		Moderate Neglect		X^2	P
	Total N	% True	Total N	% True	Total N	% True	Total N	% True		
Family routine is present	42	40.5	32	21.9	63	4.8	33	39.4	23.7	.001
Hostility and attacks on other persons	42	66.7	32	50.0	62	33.9	31	22.6	17.6	.001
Failure to keep household clean	40	52.5	32	65.6	63	87.3	33	63.6	15.8	.01
Projects on other persons	42	78.6	32	65.6	62	48.4	32	46.9	12.1	.01
Does not spontaneously express remorse in words	43	90.7	33	78.8	62	95.2	33	72.7	11.7	.01
Runs away	43	41.9	34	41.2	63	63.5	33	30.3	11.5	.01
Does not relate parental behavior with behavior of children	43	93.0	33	75.8	63	88.9	32	68.8	10.7	.02
No religious affiliation	37	67.6	29	69.0	57	91.2	27	70.4	10.2	.02
No change in behavior toward children	43	95.4	33	78.8	63	82.5	33	69.7	9.0	.05

The severe abuse and moderate neglect groups showed roughly the same proportion of families in which family routine was present. While the percentage was less than half of the total number of cases in both groups, it was conspicuously different from severe neglect. In effect, there was virtually no regular routine in the severe neglect families. The moderate abuse families were considerably more disorganized in this respect than severe abuse, but much less so than severe neglect.

The result for all groups is striking, if one considers the importance of routine in creating and maintaining any kind of family security. Continuity, the ability of parents or children to know what to expect from each other, are virtually obviated. When children lack the structural stability provided by routine, they have small means of orienting themselves to the patterns of community life. When they have no consistent expectations in the order of family life and no consistent behavior is expected from them, discipline becomes impossible.

Closely allied to routine is the item "failure to keep household clean." This item referred to the failure of parents to keep themselves and their houses to even a minimum standard of cleanliness. (Prior item, lack of cleanliness, referred to parental care of the children.) It described such behavior as that of families who used the kitchen floor as a garbage dump, or who permitted mattresses and blankets to become so filthy that it was impossible to clean them. The item did not, unfortunately, distinguish degrees of this household neglect, but at all times it described a persistent condition below a standard of cleanliness compatible with health and comfort. It was true in 52.5% of the severe abuse families and in 65.6% of moderate abuse. It was present in 87.3% of the severe neglect families and in 63.6% of moderate neglect.

The severe abuse group showed the smallest ratio of household dirtiness, and there were families in this group where the house was immaculately clean and rigidly orderly. As would be expected, severe neglect families showed the highest proportion of filthiness. In addition, the data indicated that the most extreme conditions occurred in the homes of this group. Moderate abuse and moderate neglect families were very similar on this item, and both groups showed a considerable degree of household disorganization.

Three items concerned the most common parental reactions to family crises and problems. Crises were frequent in most of these families and often involved people outside the immediate family group. A family might be evicted from their house; children might be in trouble at school; a parent might be in trouble with the law. The way the parents responded to these situations and to the persons from outside the family tended to follow certain patterns of behavior. While these patterns were not mutually exclusive, certain reactions tended to predominate.

One of these was "hostility and attacks on other persons." The parent responded to crises with a predominant attitude of antagonism and by attacking verbally (in some cases physically) the person who became involved in the situation. This was true of 66.7% of the severe abuse families and of 50.0% of the moderate abuse families. It was a typical reaction in 33.9% of the severe neglect families and in 22.6% of the moderate neglect. The distinction between abusing and neglecting families on this item is clear and sharp, and points to the greater aggressiveness of abusing families.

A related response was the item "projects on other persons." The parent blamed another person or persons for the situation, and by implication denied his own responsibility or participation in it. It would, of course, tend to justify parental hostility toward that person from the viewpoint of the parent. This was a common response in 78.6% of the severe abuse families, in 65.6% of moderate abuse, in 48.4% of severe neglect and 46.9% of moderate neglect. Again the major distinction was between abusing and neglecting families, with abuse groups showing a considerably greater tendency to project blame on others. There was very little difference on this item between severe and moderate neglect groups.

The third item concerned with parental response was "runs away." This described parental withdrawal from the whole situation and was to some degree a physical running away. This might mean a parent who left home for some period of time to escape the stressful circumstances, or who merely went to the local tavern and got drunk. The effects on the situation were likely to be much the same. It was a passive rather than aggressive response. This kind of reaction was true for 41.9% of the severe abuse, 41.2% of the moderate abuse, 63.5% of the severe neglect and 30.3% of the moderate neglect families.

It was a predominant response with the severe neglect group and accords with the pattern of confusion so conspicuous with its families. It was a much less common response with abusing groups, who did not differ on this item. The greater extent of parental responsibility of the moderate neglect group appears again in the much smaller percentage of parents who ran away from family problems and crises. In general, abusing parents tended to meet problems by blaming and attacking others. Severely neglecting parents tended to run away from them, and the parents of moderate neglect showed the greatest capacity to meet them in a more realistic form.

A common assumption noted in the case records was that these parents felt guilty about their behavior toward their children. It is an expectation that springs from what might be called a normal standard of parental behavior. In other words, caseworkers expected these parents to feel guilty because by their standard the parents ought to feel guilty. This did not obviously answer the question of whether or not that assumption was true. Since guilt is visible only in behavior that presumably reflects it, it was necessary to devise such behavioral indices. Seven were selected: (1) parents do not spontaneously express remorse in words; (2) show no change in behavior toward the children; (3) discuss their behavior without shame; (4) do not verbally relate the behavior of the children to their own behavior; (5) do not show spontaneous awareness of the unacceptability of their behavior (6) do not show awareness of unacceptability of behavior when criticized by another and, (7) do not react with self-punishment, that is, with specific responses resulting in self-damage. While it cannot be validly assumed that these indices either singly or collectively provide a reliable reflection of the presence or absence of guilt, they do provide an important indication. The behaviors themselves are important. Three of them appeared as differentiating items. The other 4 were predominantly present for the total group.

The item "A parent does not spontaneously express remorse in words" described, of course, any voluntary expressions of parental feeling. When a parent was criticized or in any way threatened because of his behavior toward his children, his expressions of regret and remorse had to be evaluated in the perspective of what he might gain or lose as a consequence. While this element of expediency cannot be totally ruled out even in spontaneous statements, there is a fair presumption that it would be less likely. The absence of such spontaneous remarks was true in 90.7% of the severe abuse families, in 78.8% of moderate abuse, in 95.2% of severe neglect families and in 72.7% of moderate neglect. The item divided along the lines of the severe as opposed to the moderate groups, and there was no distinction between neglect and abuse types. All of the families show a conspicuous absence of such expressions of feeling.

The second item "A parent does not relate parental behavior with behavior of children" described any indication that parents saw their own actions as carrying any responsibility for undesirable behavior in their children. Even when such behavior might be children going to school dirty, the question was: did parents take any responsibility for their neglect? The answer was that 93.0% of severe abuse families did not, 75.8% of moderate abuse did not, 88.9% of severe neglect and 68.8% of moderate neglect did not. Again the differences related almost entirely to degree, rather than to neglect and abuse as such.

The third item "no change in behavior toward children" is probably the most important of the group. Even when outside intervention occurred, sometimes including temporary removal of the children, there was no visible change in parental behavior. This was true for 95.4% of the severe abuse group, for 78.8% of moderate abuse, for 82.5% of the severe neglect type and for 69.7% of moderate neglect. This was most often true for severe abuse and severe neglect, and there was a considerable modification in moderate abuse and moderate neglect. Of all the groups, moderate neglect showed the greatest tendency toward change of parental behavior, although even here the proportion was not great. There was the least change among the severe abuse parents.

It should be noted that, while the other four items in this category were not differentiating ones, they were also heavily weighted against indications of guilt. The parents showed little open awareness of the unacceptability of their behavior until community criticism and intervention occurred. Even then only 38.1% of the severe abuse group indicated that this was meaningful for them.

Active affiliation with a religious body would be an encouragement toward the maintenance of some standards of behavior. The item "no religious affiliation" was an important one, since church membership could involve some measure of social control as well as respect for a standard of behavior. There was no religious affiliation, however, in 67.6% of the severe abuse families, in 69.0% of moderate abuse, in 91.2% of severe neglect families and in 70.4% of moderate neglect. It is interesting that severe neglect families were less likely to be church members than severe abuse families. The high visibility of the problems in the severe neglect group tends probably to keep them away from any standard-setting institution. When severe abuse families are outwardly well organized and visibly conforming to community standards, it is quite possible that they would more often have some religious affiliation. Moderate abuse and moderate neglect families were virtually identical on this item. Church membership was not, however, common with any of the groups.

FINDINGS ON ITEMS CHARACTERISTIC OF THE TOTAL SAMPLE

Fifteen items of the 47 that did not show significant differences by type have nevertheless relevance to the behavioral profile of the total group. The following table lists these items and gives the percentage of true responses.

ITEMS CHARACTERISTIC OF TOTAL SAMPLE

d.f. = 3 Items	Severe Abuse		Moderate Abuse		Severe Neglect		Moderate Neglect	
	Total N	% True	Total N	% True	Total N	% True	Total N	% True
Parental Indifference to Behavior of Children								
Withdrawn behavior	41	97.6	25	96.2	40	100.0	27	96.4

d.f. = 3 Items	Severe Abuse		Moderate Abuse		Severe Neglect		Moderate Neglect	
	Total N	% True	Total N	% True	Total N	% True	Total N	% True
Failure in school	23	95.8	14	100.0	35	97.2	17	89.5
Other behaviors	32	86.5	20	95.2	24	88.9	15	93.8
No consistent discipline of children	43	100.0	30	90.9	61	96.8	29	87.9
No consistent expectations of children	36	87.8	26	81.3	58	93.6	27	81.8
Children have defined responsibilities	9	22.0	8	26.7	8	13.8	6	18.8
Parental quarreling verbally	32	91.4	24	88.9	41	85.4	22	88.0
Parental fighting in presence of children	35	94.6	26	83.9	43	79.6	22	71.0
Parents share in plans	3	7.9	2	7.7	2	3.4	2	8.3
Parents share and discuss problems together	2	5.0	2	7.7	4	7.0	2	8.3
Parents share no common activities	34	85.0	22	95.7	46	83.6	22	95.7
One parent gives concrete help to other	3	7.9	4	13.3	12	21.0	6	24.0
No continuing relationship with others outside family	37	94.9	24	82.8	57	91.9	22	73.3
No consistent place in group	39	97.5	28	90.3	61	98.4	28	84.8
No initiation of responsible plan or action	38	88.4	29	87.9	61	96.8	26	78.8

These items have a practical importance for social work, which as a practicing profession must take them into account. They might also have theoretical importance, if a companion sample of families that did not physically neglect or abuse their families were available. Even in the absence of such a sample, some of them are clearly deviant from the norms and expectations of our society. All of these items showed the predominant direction of response for the total sample.

The first group of items is parental indifference to the behavior of children. Indifference was here defined as "take no action about." In other words, parents did nothing about the behavior specified. This seemed to be the only externally observable index to the emotional attitude of indifference. There was so little information on the parental attitude toward truancy, fighting and stealing by the children that no specific conclusions were possible. The data available indicated little active parental concern. The behavior of the children was itemized and the classifications were selected by 2 criteria, the behavior most likely to be common and that most likely to be externally observable. This item was not designed to provide an inclusive picture of the behavior of children from these families and focused on parental attitude to the behavior.

Truancy from school was the first of the classifications. It was true for every type, but more so for children from severe neglect families than from the other three types—16.31% for severe neglect as compared to 7.38% for moderate neglect, 8.62% for severe abuse and 8.31% for moderate abuse. Unfortunately, for 53.85% of the families there was no information on this item. It would seem a fair assumption that the actual extent of truancy is very high among the children in these families, and that it tends to be higher in the severe neglect group. The indifference of the parents toward this is clear.

Fighting was the next category of behavior. It was true of children in all types, but since on 55% of the families there was no information, it is difficult to know how serious or how extensive the problem was. The item itself did not attempt to specify the kind or degree of fighting, although it was not noted as true unless it represented a consistent pattern of behavior. The data when available reflected a pattern of quarreling among children both within and outside of the family that much exceeded what could be considered the normal degree. The parents tended to ignore this and at times, particularly in the abusing families, seemed even to encourage it.

Parental indifference to stealing was true for the total group, although this result must be heavily qualified by the fact that on 72% of the families there was no information. This may reflect a relative absence of such behavior on the part of the children, or thefts of a sufficiently minor character to evade official notice. It is probable that both explanations have some validity. What data was available indicated that the children in these families when they did steal tended to commit minor, rather impulsive thefts, to take advantage of impromptu opportunities rather than to create and organize such situations. Like their parents, the children tended toward impulsive rather than organized or planned action. Parents tended to ignore this behavior and to deny it when it was officially recognized by outsiders. In a number of cases there were indications that parents encouraged it, and only when the children were caught was the parental reaction critical.

Interestingly, withdrawn behavior was more frequently observed and recorded than the more aggressive actions. Whether withdrawn behavior was more common than aggressive actions or more commonly observed by the caseworkers is not clear. What was strikingly clear was the parental indifference to it. Since it did not involve parents with any coercive agency such as the police, they remained in any observable sense virtually oblivious to the child's withdrawal from contacts with other people and from activities and interests. The apathy and depression of these children was a stark reality that contrasted sharply with the energy and initiative of more normal children.

Failure in school was also regarded with indifference by parents in all the types. As with the withdrawn behavior, parents seemed to be oblivious to the fact that it had any importance or meaning. The data revealed that they were aware of it, but they were obviously not concerned about it. One would expect the rate of school failure to be high among the children in this group, and so far as it was recorded this was substantiated. However, on 48.92% of the families there was no information. There is no good explanation of why this information was not acquired and recorded. Logically, there was little incentive for these children to succeed at school, and the high incidence of physical neglect would further handicap any efforts they might make.

A final, catchall category, simply called "other," was included to cover types of behavior not previously specified. The most conspicuous behavior that emerged here was sexual activities. The parental reaction was again indifference for the most part. In some cases sex activity was encouraged, particularly when it was instrumental in bringing some material rewards to the family. In some of the abusing families, there was violent opposition on the part of one parent to even casual contacts by a child with anyone of the opposite sex. This was most noticeable in the attitude of some of the fathers toward an adolescent daughter, when the girl was forbidden any social contacts with boys on the assumption that these would inevitably involve sexual relations. Interestingly, when a girl did defy the paternal prohibition with success, the parent tended to revert to indifference and to ignore her completely.

To sum up this whole group of items, parents tended to be indifferent to all the behavior of their children. Their reactions arose not in relation to the behavior but in response to community criticism, and more specifically to community pressure. Under these circumstances, parental reaction tended to be denial of the reality of the behavior or denial of responsibility for it. In effect, the children's behavior was their affair, not the parents'.

Three items that are closely interrelated and that describe parental behavior in establishing standards for children are "no consistent discipline of children," "no consistent expectations of children," and "children have defined responsibilities." Discipline is consistent instruction and must conform with some established rules or standards. Whatever the nature of those standards, they must have continuity. It was precisely the lack of such consistent rules that left the children of these families without guides or discipline. This was just as true of abuse as of neglect families. It appeared, in fact, in 100% of the severe abuse group and 96.8% of severe neglect.

Despite the emphasis on punishment in abusing families, there was the same lack of consistent rules for behavior. In other words, parental punishment of children was divorced from the specific behavior of the children. It became, in effect, punishment for its own sake. The severity and brutality of parental abuse and its lack of corrective purpose distinguish it clearly from the customary concept of punishment of children.

The reasons which parents in the severe abuse group gave as explanations for their behavior further illumine this difference. The answers could be roughly classified under seven headings; (1) do not feel the child belongs to the family; (2) the children don't obey (specific examples include such things as five minutes late getting home from school); (3) parents hate the children; (4) the children wet and soil; (5) the children are "crazy" or "evil" or "freaks"; (6) the children drive the parent "crazy"; (7) bizarre incidents, such as "child washed the milk bottle." It should be noted that explanations as such were given by parents only when their behavior was questioned by someone outside the family. The lack of relevance between the behavior of the child and the savagery of the punishment was not noted by any parent, nor was any specific pattern of child disobedience described by the parents. In fact, the most striking common factor in all the answers was their inappropriateness as rational explanations. The disparity between the described behavior of the children and the nature of the parental punishment was of overwhelming proportion.

It should be noted here that in seven of the severe abuse families parental abuse was confined to one child only. The other children were neglected but not abused. Further, the other children in the family were encouraged to discriminate against this one child, and were permitted to abuse and torment him. In one case, parental feeling toward one child was so extreme that they finally attempted to kill him. When the boy was removed from the home, he had to be hospitalized both for severe physical injuries and for extreme malnutrition. The other children, while neglected, were in no sense in a comparable physical condition. It is not clear why just one child should be singled out for this extreme rejection and abuse. The parents themselves sometimes said that he was "different," did not "belong" to them. Occasionally a parent identified him with some adult that the parent had hated, usually a parent or stepparent of his own. In one case a father abused his daughter and ignored his son. There was no clear or consistent pattern, however, to explain why this one particular child was selected as the focus for parental hatred. More detailed observation by caseworkers might contribute needed data toward the solution of this question. It would, for instance, be important to know whether, upon the removal of the abused child from the family, another child is then selected as the victim. Data on this were lacking in the records.

The item "no consistent expectations for children" further defined the lack of consistent standards of behavior. When children have no clear assurance of what, if anything, is expected of them and of what they in turn may expect from parents, the result can only be chaos. In a sense, the item "children have defined responsibilities" is redundant. It was true in less than a quarter of the cases in all of the groups. Even when children did have some defined duties, these tended to be confined to areas convenient for the parents, such as baby-sitting, and were often inconsistent in extent and duration. This is probably the explanation for the disparity in response between this item and the one concerned with consistent expectations. In some of the families, responsibilities of one or more of the children were defined by an older child, and tended to endure only so long as the age of the child or the nature of the circumstances promoted this.

Another group of items concerned the incompatibility of the parents and their lack of sharing as marital partners. "Quarrelling verbally" was common with the parents of all four types. The endless bickering and mutual hostility were an integral part of the climate of these homes. The item "fighting in presence of children" was a further indication of this. It was also predominantly true of all groups. It is not surprising that there was little sharing between the parents.

The items "parents share in plans," "parents share and discuss problems together," and "parents share no common activities" were depressingly similar in results. Parents did not plan together and did not see their problems as mutual, rather than individual. They shared few activities, either in the area of work or of recreation.

The accompanying item "one parent gives concrete help to the other partner" showed the same lack of mutual concern and loyalty. This whole group of items depicts families with little inner unity or organization. Marital roles are to a large extent nonexistent. The parents live together as enemies, who seem to blame each other for the family misery, but have little awareness of how each contributes to it.

Nor were the families in this sample able to achieve stability through their relationships with people outside the nuclear family group. The item "no continuing relationships with others outside the family" was predominantly true of every group. Whether such other people were relatives, neighbors or transient friends, the parental relationships tended to be sporadic, brief and superficial. Occasionally, one parent would develop a rather intensive relationship with a neighbor or acquaintance, and this might endure for several weeks or even months. With monotonous regularity, such friendships ended in a violent quarrel and ensuing bitterness. It is interesting that in many such situations the friendship was hostile toward the parent not involved in it. Relatives were sometimes not seen for long periods of time, or were approached only when a family crisis precipitated a special need. In some families, relatives visited more frequently, but these visits tended to end in quarrels and periods of separation.

Parental connections with the outside community are sharply delineated by the response to the item "membership in an organized group." Out of the total sample, at least 85.00% of every group showed no membership or participation in such a group. While church membership was listed as a separate item, the response was the same failure to participate in or to belong to an organized group. This result has particular implications for a group-conscious society such as this one.

Sociological studies have consistently found that participation in organized groups is class-related, and that the lower economic group tends to participate less than the middle class. Reissman[1] found significant difference in church attendance and organization membership between high and low class groups, particularly when class was defined by the variable occupational prestige. Warner[1] noted in *The Social Life of a Modern Community* that "As the class rank increases, the proportion of its members who belong to associations also increases; and as the position of a class decreases, the percentage of those who belong to associations decreases." This would be consistent with the findings on the families in this sample.

This lack of participation by these families emphasizes both their solitariness and their absence of any established place in the larger social structure. Even in the absence of meaningful human relationships, an established status or participation in a continuing group can provide important structural support for greater personal organization, but the parents lacked this support also. Not even in the common, informal neighborhood activities were they participants. While the item was intentionally restricted to continuing membership in a group, the data indicated that even sporadic and tenuous participation tended to be lacking. The extent of the social isolation of these families must clearly have implications of considerable importance.

The prevailing passivity of all these familes is apparent in the results for the item "no initiation of responsible plan or action." It was over 75% true of every group. The actions that were taken by these parents tended to be impulsive and in response to some pressure. They were not often initiated by the parents as something they wanted or planned to do. Further, they were not often a part of any consistent plan. Actions tended to be isolated fragments, separated from any clear purpose or ongoing plan. As a group, the families in this sample lacked goals, continuity and ordered structure for daily life.

[1]Leonard Reissman, "Class, Leisure and Social Participation," *American Sociological Review* 19, n. 1, February, 1954.

[1]W. Lloyd Warner and Paul S. Lunt, *The Social Life of a Modern Community*, p. 329, (New Haven: Yale University Press, 1941).

Two items that are in addition to the fifteen cited in this chapter are included here, even though information was lacking on them in a high percentage of the cases. They are "sexual activities in the presence of the children" and "sexual activities with children." They are included here because the data indicated that they may represent behaviors far more frequent in these families than the recorded information reveals. Their importance in family interaction is self-evident. "Sexual activities in the presence of the children" was reported true in 22 of the 108 families where information was recorded. Eight of these were in severe abuse, 9 in moderate abuse, 4 in severe neglect and 1 in moderate neglect. This item did not refer to the accidental witnessing of parental intercourse by children, but to overt sexual activities by a parent in the presence of the children. These activities could be between the parents, or between one parent and a person outside the family. In either case, the deliberate exposure of children of varying ages to adult sexual relations implies a degree of breakdown in family values and standards that is of major significance. It warrants much more detailed study than has yet been given it. There is a good probability that this may be a key item in evaluating the degree of family and individual disintegration.

Related to this is the item "sexual activities with children." While this was reported true in only 5.0% of the families, by definition in the abuse group, this figure does require some further clarification. It was not marked true unless there was conclusive evidence (such as parental admission that this was so), but there were often indications in the records of incestuous activities. Whether these were overt statements by the children, oblique remarks by the parents or parental attitudes such as those of the fathers cited previously, they were rarely pursued by the caseworkers and hence remain inconclusive. Given the vital importance in any society of the incest taboo, it would seem of primary significance to devise means of learning the extent of incestuous relations in these families. There were sufficient indications in the records to cast doubt on the validity of the figure given in this study.

Bibliography

Ackerman, Nathan. *The Psychodynamics of Family Life* (New York: Basic Books, Inc. 1958).

Adelson, Lester. "Slaughter of the Innocents—A Study of Forty-six Homicides in which the Victims Were Children," *The New England Journal of Medicine* 264, n. 26, pp. 1345–1349, June 29, 1961.

Angell, Robert Cooley. *The Family Encounters the Depression* (New York: Charles Scribner's Sons, 1936).

Anshen, Ruth (Ed.). *The Family, Its Functions and Destiny* (New York: Harper & Brothers, 1949).

Bakwin, Harry. "Multiple Skeletal Lesions in Young Children Due to Trauma," *Journal of Pediatrics*, 49, n. 1, pp. 7–16, July 1956.

Bell, Norman W. and Ezra F. Vogel, (Eds.). *A Modern Introduction to the Family* (Glencoe, Illinois: The Free Press, 1960).

Bloch, Herbert A. *Disorganization, Personal and Social* (New York: Alfred A. Knopf, 1952).

Boardman, Helen E. "A Project to Rescue Children from Inflicted Injuries," *Social Work* 7, n. 1, January 1962.

Boehm, Bernice, "An Assessment of Family Adequacy in Protective Cases," *Child Welfare* XLI, n. 1, January 1962.

Brody, Sylvia. *Patterns of Mothering* (New York: International Universities Press, 1956).

Buell, Bradley and Associates. *Community Planning for Human Services* (New York: Columbia University Press, 1952).

Burgess, E. W. and H. J. Locke. *The Family: From Institution to Companionship* (2nd ed.) (New York: American Book Company, 1953).

Cavan, Ruth Shouls and Katherine Howland Ranck. *The Family and the Depression* (Chicago, Illinois: The University of Chicago Press, 1938).

Child Welfare League Pamphlet. *Standards for Child Protective Service* (New York, 1960).

Children's Division, The American Humane Association, Publication. *Protective Services and Community Expectations* (Denver, Colorado, 1961).

Termination of Parental Rights (Denver, Colorado, 1961).

Protecting the Battered Child (Denver, Colorado, 1962).

Guidelines for Legislation to Protect the Battered Child (Denver, Colorado, 1963).

Child Abuse (Denver, Colorado, 1963).

Conference on Economic Progress Publication. *Poverty and Deprivation in the United States* (Washington, D.C., 1962).

Dick, Kenneth and Lydia J. Strand. "The Multi-problem Family and Problems of Service," *Social Casework* XXXIX, n. 6, pp. 349–355, June 1958.

Elmer, Elizabeth. "Abused Young Children Seen in Hospitals," *Journal of Social Work* 5, n. 4, October 1960.

Fisher, S. H. "Skeletal Manifestations of Parent-induced Trauma in Infants and Children," *Southern Medical Journal* 51, pp. 956–960, August 1958.

Fliess, Dr. Robert. *Ego and Body Ego* (New York: Schulte Publishing Co., 1961).

Freeman, Henry. "Applying Family Diagnosis in Practice," *Social Service Review* XXXIV, n. 1, pp. 32–41, March 1960.

Geismar, Ludwig L. "The Multi-problem Family—Significance of Research Findings," *Social Welfare Forum, 1960, National Conference on Social Welfare* pp. 166–179, (New York: Columbia University Press, 1960).

Geismar, Ludwig L. "Similarity and Variance in the Application of Standardized Family Diagnosis," (unpublished paper, based on research data from studies at Graduate School of Social Work, Rutgers University, 1961).

Geismar, Ludwig L. and Beverly Ayres. *Families in Trouble—An Analysis of the Basic Social Characteristics of 100 Families Served by the Project* (St. Paul: Family Centered Project, 1958).

——*Patterns of Change in Problem Families—A Study of Social Functioning and Movement in 150 Closed Cases* (St. Paul: Family Centered Project, 1959).

——*Measuring Family Functioning—A Manual on a Method of Evaluating the Social Functioning of Disorganized Families* (St. Paul: Family Centered Project, 1960).

Gibbins, T. C. N. and A. Walker. *Cruel Parents* (London: Institute for the Study and Treatment of Delinquency, 1956).

Gross, Mason and McEachern. *Explorations in Role Analysis* (New York: John Wiley & Sons, 1958).

Groves, Ernest. *The Family and Its Social Functions* (Chicago: J. B. Lippincott Co., 1940).

Gwinn, John L., Kenneth W. Lewis, and Herbert G. Peterson, Jr. "Roentgenographic Manifestations of Unsuspected Trauma in Infancy," *Journal of the American Medical Association* 176, n. 11, pp. 926–929, June 17, 1961.

Haas, Walter. "Reaching Out—A Dynamic Concept in Casework," *Social Work* 4, n. 3, pp. 41–46, July 1959.

Hallinan, Helen W. "Coordinating Agency Efforts in Behalf of the Hard-to-reach Family," *Social Casework* XL, pp. 9–17, January 1959.

Hancock, Claire. "Digest of a Study of Protective Services and the Problem of Neglect of Children in New Jersey," State of New Jersey, Department of Institutions and Agencies, State Board of Child Welfare (Trenton, New Jersey, 1958).

Harman, Harry H. *Modern Factor Analysis* (Chicago: University of Chicago Press, 1960).

Henry, Charlotte S. "Motivation in Non-voluntary Clients," *Social Casework* XXXIX, n. 2-3, pp. 130–137, February-March 1958.

Hill, Reuben. *Families Under Stress* (New York: Harper & Brothers, 1949).

Hill, Reuben. "Generic Features of Families Under Stress," *Social Casework* XXXIX, n. 2-3, pp. 139–150, February-March 1958.

Hollingshead, August B. "Class Differences in Family Stability," *The Annals of the American Academy of Political and Social Science* 272, pp. 39–46, November 1950.

Hollingshead, August B. "Class Differences in Family Stability," in *Social Perspectives on Behavior*, Herman D. Stein and Richard A. Cloward, (Eds.).

Hollingshead, August B. and Frederick C. Redlich. *Social Class and Mental Illness: A Community Study* (New York: John Wiley & Sons, Inc., 1958).

Hollis, Florence. *Women in Marital Conflict* pp. 83–84 (New York: Family Service Association of America, 1949).

Hyman, Herbert H. "The Value Systems of Different Classes," in *Social Perspectives on Behavior*, Herman D. Stein and Richard A. Cloward, (Eds.).

Kahn, Alfred. *Children in Trouble* (Citizen's Committee for Children of New York City, 1957).

——*Protecting New York City's Children* (Citizen's Committee for Children of New York City, 1960).

——*New York City Schools and Children Who Need Help* (Citizen's Committee for Children of New York City, 1962).

——*Planning Community Services for Children in Trouble* (New York: Columbia University Press, 1963).

Kluckhohn, Clyde. "Culture and Behavior," in *Handbook of Social Psychology*, Gardner Lindzey (Ed.), Vol. II (Cambridge: Addison-Wesley Press, Inc., 1954).

Kluckhohn, Florence and John P. Spiegel. *Integration and Conflict in Family Behavior*, The Committee on the Family of the Group for the Advancement of Psychiatry (Topeka, Kansas: August 1954).

Kluckhohn, Florence. "Dominant and Variant Value Orientations" in *Personality in Nature, Society and Culture,* Clyde Kluckhohn, Henry A. Murray and David Schnieder (Eds.) (New York: Alfred A. Knopf, 1953).

Koos, Earl Loman. *Families in Trouble* (New York: King's Crown Press, 1946).

Lewis, Hylan, Ph.D. *Child Rearing Practices Among Low Income Families,* Casework Papers, 1961.

Lindenberg, Ruth Ellen. "Hard to Reach: Client or Casework Agency?" *Social Work* 3, n. 4, pp. 27–28, October 1958.

Maas, Henry S. and Richard E. Engler, Jr. *Children in Need of Parents* (New York: Columbia University Press, 1959).

Marcuse, Bert. "The Multi-problem Family—Its Challenge," *The Social Worker* 28, pp. 48–57, January 1960.

Merton, Robert K. *Social Theory and Social Structure* (Glencoe, Illinois: The Free Press, 1949).

Mowrer, Ernest R. *Family Disorganization* (Chicago: The University of Chicago Press, 1939).

Mulford, Robert M., Victor B. Wylegala, and Elwood F. Melson. *Case-worker and Judge in Neglect Cases* (New York: Child Welfare League of America, Inc., 1956).

Murdock, George P. *Social Structure* (New York: The MacMillan Co., 1949).

National Association of Social Workers, New York City Chapter. *Multi-problem Families and Casework Practice* (New York, June 1960) (mimeographed).

New York City Youth Board. *Reaching the Unreached* (New York, 1952).

——*How They Were Reached—A Study of 310 Children and Their Families Known to Referral Units,* Monograph No. 2, November 1954.

——*Reaching the Unreached Family—A Study of Service to Families and Children,* Monograph No. 5, 1958.

Norman, F. M. "The Skills Needed for Work with Problem Families," *Social Work* 10, n. 1, pp. 764–765, January 1953.

Ormsby, Ralph. "Defining the Problem Family," *Social Work* 4, n. 1, p. 109, January 1959.

Overton, Alice. "Taking Help from Our Clients," *Social Work* 5, n. 2, pp. 42–50, April 1960.

——"Serving Families Who Don't Want Help," *Social Casework* XXXIV, n. 7, pp. 304–309, July 1953.

Overton, Alice, Katherine H. Tinker and Associates. *Casework Notebook, 1957* (A reporting and description of casework techniques and experience in the project).

Page, Miriam O. "Cohesion, Dignity and Hope for Multi-problem Families," *Children,* March-April 1961.

Parsons, Talcott. *The Social System* (Glencoe, Illinois: The Free Press, 1951).

Parsons, Talcott and Robert F. Bales. *Family Socialization and Inter-action Process* (Glencoe, Illinois: The Free Press, 1955).

Philip, A. F. and Noel Timms. *The Problem of the "Problem Family,"* Family Service Units (London, 1957).

Pollak, Otto. "A Family Diagnosis Model," *Social Service Review* XXXIV, n. 1, pp. 19–31, March 1960.

Polier, Honorable Justine W. *Orphans with Parents—Parental Rights in the Law and the Courts* (unpublished paper).

Queen, Stuart and John B. Adams. *The Family in Various Cultures* (New York: J. B. Lippincott Company, 1952).

Reissman, Leonard. *Class in American Society* (Glencoe, Illinois: The Free Press, 1961).

Roney, Jay L. "Special Stresses on Low Income Families," *Social Case-work* 39, n. 2-3, pp. 150–158, February-March 1958.

Silver, Henry K. and C. Henry Kempe. "The Problem of Parental Criminal Neglect and Severe Physical Abuse of Children," (unpublished paper read at annual meeting of the American Pediatric Society, May 1959).

Silverman, F. N. "The Roentgen Manifestations of Unrecognized Skeletal Trauma in Infants," *American Journal of Roentgenology, Radium Therapy and Nuclear Medicine* 69, pp. 413–427, March 1953.

——*Unrecognized Trauma—A Medical Social Problem* (presented at Detroit Children's Alumni Association, April 1958).

State Charities Aid Association. *Multi-problem Families: A New Name or a New Problem* (New York, May 1960).

Stott, D. H. *Unsettled Children and Their Families* (London: University of London Press, 1956).

Strickland, Evalyn M. "Helping the Multi-problem Family Through Coordination of Services in a Predominantly Rural Setting," *Child Welfare* XLI, n. 1, January 1962.

Toby, Jackson. "The Differential Impact of Family Disorganization," *American Sociological Review* 22, n. 5, pp. 505–512, October 1957.

U.S. Department of Health, Education and Welfare, Children's Bureau. *The Abused Child* (Washington, D.C., 1963).

Welfare Council of Metropolitan Chicago. *ADC: Facts, Fallacies, Future* (Chicago, Illinois).

Whale, Margaret. "The Problem Family—The Case for Social Casework," *Social Work* II, n. 1, pp. 881–887, January 1954.

Willie, Charles V. "The Structure and Composition of 'Problem' and 'Stable' Families in a Lower Income Population" (unpublished paper based on findings of Ford Foundation Project at Syracuse University Youth Development Center, 1961).

Wiltse, Kermit. "The Hopeless Family," *Social Welfare Forum 1958* (New York: Columbia University Press, 1958).

Women's Group on Public Welfare. *The Neglected Child and His Family* (New York: Oxford University Press, 1948).

Index